NEAR DEATH
LESSONS

A Dream. A Terminal Illness.
An Extraordinary Life Gained
From 8 Near Death Experiences

CHRIS JANKULOVSKI

Published by
BEVERLY HILLS PUBLISHING
468 Camden Drive

Beverly Hills, California 90210

Beverly Hills Publishing Inc.
www.beverlyhillspublishing.com

ISBN: 979-8-9861550-4-3

Dedication

To my loving wife, Rica, and sons, Jay and
Billy, whom I adore.

Table of Contents

Introduction

I began writing this book after I came home from my second brain operation in September 2016. I was expecting to be out of the hospital after five days, carrying on with life. Instead, the hospital advised me to go to a rehabilitation center and stay there for months.

I was in bad shape. I was experiencing extreme fatigue and couldn't get out of bed, let alone sit on a chair for more than ten minutes before I had to go back to bed again. I needed constant care. I couldn't feed myself; I couldn't breathe or talk properly. The left side of my body didn't work.

I told myself that as soon as I could sit on my chair for an hour, I would start writing this book so I could share my story. It had been on my mind for years, but unfortunately, it took a second brain operation for me to wake up to the realization that if I didn't start writing it, I may never get the chance to do so. But I'm getting ahead of myself. Let me take you back to how this all began …

"You have a hereditary condition called Von Hippel-Lindau syndrome," the specialist told me. "The life expectancy of people with this condition is thirty years of age. You are going to have cancers all over your body throughout your life." After a pause, he added, "You might even have cancer now." His bedside manner was brutal.

I stared at him from across his desk, not knowing what to say. I had so many questions. I *could* have cancer? Where? I'll be dead by thirty? How can that be? How do you know?

I was nineteen and getting the results of blood tests to determine what was causing a blurry spot in the middle of my right eye.

Back in my car, I cried. At home, my devastated parents tried to talk to me, but I felt as if my life was already over. I cried for two weeks.

At the end of my teen years, after a childhood and adolescence where I'd often questioned how I was going to fit in to the life expected of me, this bombshell diagnosis shook me to my core and changed my attitude to life.

There's an Australian rock band called Midnight Oil, with a song titled "Power and the Passion," about not living your life on your knees. I embraced its message. If I had just ten years more, what was the point in doing something I didn't like? I didn't want to be on my knees begging for life.

I stopped believing in the future. What was the point of preparing for the future if I didn't have one? I rebelled and did the craziest things—drinking and smoking dope, traveling the world, and having noncommittal relationships, and not really caring about anyone or anything because of my "death sentence."

In addition to not caring about my future, I didn't understand why it was still important for me to have a career and to make my life matter and count in some way. Unable to find a job I enjoyed, I decided to be an entrepreneur. This was hard for my father to understand, because he was used to working for someone all his life. My relatives and high school friends in Melbourne often challenged me: "Who do you think you are?"

I struggled and clawed my way through life against all odds. I became a risk-taker, a mover, and a shaker, and had many successes and failures in my early business life.

A decade later, a series of near-death experiences, including my first deadly brain tumor diagnosis and operation in June 2005, triggered a profound positive personal transformation and finally led me to live the life of my dreams.

My adversities thus became the catalyst for my transformation at the age of thirty-two. From someone who didn't know what he wanted out of life, I became someone with no shortage of goals. I didn't have any more time to entertain worry, fear, or self-doubt. I just went all-in committing to everything I wanted to do. My passion for life was ignited.

We all know how one near death experience can transform someone's life. In my case, I had a total of 8 near death experiences. What's unique about me is that I've achieved all my successes *because of* my adverse medical diagnoses. Throughout my journey, I share how these experiences transformed my life into ideas about how to live life to the fullest. I have done a lot of work reflecting on these ideas and have distilled them into five life lessons. I refer to these as my story unfolds, and you'll find them explained later in the book.

Hence, the title of the book: *Near-Death Lessons*. This is a true story of my journey from being a young man who didn't believe in the future to a person who now strives to make his life count in every way he can even though his tomorrows are not guaranteed. I'm in very good spirits after what I've endured and look forward to living my life every day. I'm still here, I'm still alive, and I do all I can to make the most of my time.

Those who may have confronted their own serious adversities or challenges in life and can't see hope in their tomorrows may find my attitude refreshing and my journey inspirational. I choose to maintain tremendous enthusiasm for my future and I hope my story empowers you to keep going in the face of whatever adversity you may be confronting in life.

CHAPTER 1

Not a Typical Kid

I was born in 1973 into a typical immigrant family, but as a kid there was nothing typical about me. I knew there was more to life than working hard for other people and just getting by. I knew there had to be a better way and I was determined to find it.

My parents, Bill and Vera, were born in Macedonia but met when they immigrated to Australia. They were swept into a whirlwind romance, marrying a month after they met. There was no fuss in those days, no mucking around, because after another month, Mum was pregnant with me. She was young, twenty, when she gave birth to me. Dad was five years older.

Early on we lived in Carlton, an inner suburb of Melbourne, Australia. Carlton is a popular Italian-influenced area with coffee shops and restaurants lining the streets. My earliest memory is of Dad and me driving to the hospital when I was two years old to visit Mum who had just given birth to my sister. We drove an old, beat-up car, and I remember resting my little arms along the top of the crinkly vinyl car seat babbling on about my new baby sister.

I was very excited when my sister, Petra, entered our lives but little did I know that our home would become a battlefront and she would become the enemy by the time I was six. If we were in the same room, we'd try to kill each other. Petra and I were opposites. She was a good girl who did what was expected of her by family and society. I was the rebel, the one causing my parents to go gray before their time.

Dad had a strong work ethic. In other words, he was a bloody hard worker. Early in his career, he became the manager at ATCO, a rapidly growing factory producing electrical light transformers and similar products. He was always trying to look after his own by placing Macedonians or Yugoslavs into jobs at the factory and helping them get settled. It wasn't until later in life that I realized my dad was helping other immigrants settle into a new life in Australia by providing the jobs. Over the years, there were many people who my dad helped to start their lives in Australia. They were very grateful for the opportunities he provided.

Dad was on the cusp of moving from working class to middle class, and at the age of eleven, that impressed me. At one point, he was the manager of one thousand employees in the factory and business was thriving, but he always remained an employee.

My mum worked from home, assembling electrical components from the company Dad worked for. The electrical components came in boxes and my mum often referred to her work as "boxes." It was ideal for her because she could look after us, watch television and get paid. She loved to chit-chat with family and her Macedonian friends and was a great cook. I think she was happy with her life.

I started public primary school in Lalor, north of Melbourne. Right from the beginning I fell behind. Reading, writing, and comprehension were a real challenge. I vividly remember sitting on the mat with the other kids listening to the teacher and not under-standing her. It was as if she was speaking another language. She was speaking English, but I was puzzled as to *why* I couldn't under-stand her and everyone else could.

I put my hand up to ask for help, but the teacher said, "I'll get back to you." I don't remember getting any help. It was frustrating and strange because I felt as though there was something wrong with me. They were speaking my language, but I had no idea what was going on. The class was racing along, and I was stuck at the beginning, lost in confusion. I had to repeat my first year of school, which set a bad tone for my entire school life.

I believed that I was a slow learner. I must have been dyslexic but was never formally diagnosed. I had to psych myself up to pay attention or to concentrate on reading. It was a real problem for me.

When I was younger, I never imagined I'd confront major health adversities as an adult and have several near-death experi-ences. But when I was seven, I encountered the first of these.

My first near-death experience

I had a vivid dream in which my cousins and I were playing hide-and-seek in a clothing store while my mum was shopping. We ran in and out of the circular racks of clothing, making a mess. I hid inside the folds of clothes where it was dark, but my feet were visi-ble at the bottom where a stripe of white light fell across my toes. I stepped back into the shadows of the clothing and dreamed that I fell back into a kind of black hole. I was plunging into the shadow of darkness, freefalling as if I'd jumped out of a plane. I fell for a

long time, screaming all the way down, until a faceless, nude mannequin embraced and cradled me just before I hit the bottom.

I woke up screaming with incredible pains in my belly. My parents rushed me to the hospital where the doctors discovered my
appendix had burst. They said I was very lucky to be alive and I
had to stay in hospital for two weeks. I always felt that I had been
saved, though. It may have presented as a faceless mannequin in
my dreams, but I believe I was caught by the arms of an angel. I
believe it was more than a dream.

Toward the end of my high school years we moved seven kilometers away from Gladstone Park to Greenvale, on the cusp of
suburbia next to the wide-open country landscape. It had nice big
homes, but it felt like we were stuck out in the middle of nowhere.
We had to get rides or catch public transport to school or the
shops. As I got older and started socializing, it was just too far from
where the action was. It was twenty kilometers away from Melbourne City.

When I was fourteen, my dad got me my first job. It was the
same job that my mother had, assembling parts from the factory
where my dad worked. I had to thread a copper wire the length of
a pencil through eight rings. At the factory, they would cut the wire
to remove the rings and use them for various electrical assemblies.
I wrapped the copper wires together, sealed them and put them
in a box. Every box had hundreds of these rings, and I was paid a
certain amount per box. It was good money for a kid my age. I was
making a couple of thousands of dollars a month, and back in the
1980s that was a significant amount of money. It was my first taste
of having money. At fourteen years old, I felt like a millionaire.

On the one hand, I was feeling empowered as a "millionaire" at fourteen; I was also experiencing the opposite at school. You could say that I had a bad attitude toward school. I followed the rules just enough to pass and not get kicked out, but the school system didn't work for me. For example, in Year 10, a schoolmate and I would often avoid most of the math classes all year by hiding somewhere in the school or going to the shopping center nearby. Toward the end of the school season, I worked my ass off for two full days over a weekend, learning the whole math curriculum just before the end-of-year exams. I studied very hard for those two days. To my surprise, I passed and did well. My teacher was surprised also but failed me because of my dismal attendance. I still hold a grudge.

I didn't even bother studying for my accounting class in Year 10. I didn't want to take the exam but was forced to. I put my head on the desk and went to sleep.

"Are you seriously not going to attempt the exam?" my teacher asked.

"No."

"Alright, then get the hell out of here," she yelled at me.

I was delighted. "Done. I'm out." I woke up in a sleepy state and was delighted to be able to leave.

I was constantly mocking the school system, spending much of my time with the principal, who always threatened me with suspension. Even though I wanted a better education, school just wasn't for me. I don't know whether it was because of my suspected dyslexia or because I was bored, but I felt it was a big waste of time, except for physical education, art, science and the girls, of course.

It was while I was cramming for my math exam over that one weekend I first noticed a problem with my eyes. A section of the book had a blurry spot, which I never saw before. I kept rubbing my eyes and thinking there was something in my eye. When I went away from desk in my bedroom, I noticed it was still blurry. That's when I realized I had a problem.

The first thing I did was tell my dad. "Dad, I think I have something wrong with my eye. It's blurry." Dad was the one who arranged for me to see the doctor, and he drove me to the appointment.

At sixteen, I was diagnosed with angiomas—tumors in the eye. At risk of going blind, I underwent laser surgeries to remove the angiomas at the back of the retina in my right eye. Between the ages of sixteen and nineteen I had many laser treatments on that eye, and this weakened my lower eyelid muscles, making my right eye look bigger than the left. I was extremely self-conscious about this and felt it was destroying my life. I tried many things to correct it, such as squeezing my facial muscles to balance out my eyes, but to no avail.

Teenage years are hard enough with the usual hormonal issues and other changes, but now after the laser treatments I had my eye to worry about as well. It made me really shy around girls. I tried not to look at them directly. I wondered what they thought of me and if they found me attractive or not.

When I went out, I'd position myself at an angle or stand sideways so people wouldn't look at my bigger eye. Who was I kidding? Everyone noticed the difference in my eyes, and my efforts couldn't hide it. When I met someone and shook their hand, I couldn't look them in the eye, which is a big deal for a man. Looking someone in the eye is about having integrity, being open and honest, and I couldn't do that. I hated myself for it, but I didn't want anyone to see the slight deformity in my right eye.

I had visual distortion but no physical pain in my eye. But it was the emotional pain—self-inflicted—that got to me. I felt sorry for myself and played the blame game well, "winning" as a victim every time. My self-esteem was low, and I didn't feel like I could really be me.

My eye issues were a real "eye-opener" for me (pardon the pun). My eye doctor insisted I see a psychologist to help me deal with my self-esteem issues. The psychologist recommended that I talk to a plastic surgeon to "fix" my eye so that I could feel better about myself. The surgeon was a flashy little dude who looked perfect, almost plastic.

He said something like, "We'll cut an incision under your mouth and stitch it to your eyelid. You should recover within three to four months." I shook my head in disbelief. While I was desperate to change the look of my eye, the operation sounded horrific.

I had a choice: have the operation or change my thinking and accept my eye. No one presented me with that choice. Because of the possibility of a horrific operation, I had no other alternative than to confront this reality.

It was an incredibly hard decision, considering how much I believed my eye was ruining my life, but I chose to accept my eye, or at least try to change my thinking about it. Though I was 25 percent visually impaired at the time, I could still see. I questioned why I would have an operation just to make my eyes look even. I didn't want to undergo some painful medical procedure with all the months of healing.

But changing my thinking wasn't easy. Accepting my eye wasn't easy. I still avoided looking people in the eye, still avoided girls, and still avoided looking in the mirror.

It took years for me to accept that I couldn't change my eye. I was twenty-two when I made the choice to stop making my eye a problem in my life. I realized it was all about how I *perceived* the situation. Jesus, why had I made my life so hard for myself all those years? All this time I'd had a choice. It was the first time in my life where I changed the way I had been thinking about it all along. I don't need to have the operation to change. How profound is that? I had no idea that I could change. It turns out, the problem I thought was the problem was not the problem at all.

Looking back, I can see that self-inflicted injuries are worse than the angiomas and laser treatments I had with my eye. Over time, I found the answer to my eye problems, and it was simply that I had a choice to look at things differently—with fresh eyes.

By changing my perspective and the meaning around situations, I could change my life, just like that. After many years of suffering, I was able to turn my thinking around and appreciate my bigger eye more than my smaller eye. I found positive reinforcements in various readings about the beauty of bigger eyes. Big eyes are seen as attractive in many cultures, and I started to now lead with my big eye whenever I would meet someone for the first time. Talk about a complete switch! Before, I was hiding my larger eye; now I was leading with it.

By flipping my way of thinking about my eye as attractive instead of unattractive, my anxieties and personal self-esteem issues were flipped around. I went from photos facing away my big eye to showing my big eye to the camera.

But you know what? I don't care what books or the media or anyone says, because now I love both my eyes as they are. Changing the way you think about a situation is such a great technique to apply to any health or life issue you have.

What I noticed was the moment I stopped making my eye issue an issue, other people no longer brought it up. At the end of the day, I'm living with me for the rest of my life. These people who made comments are not living with me 24-7. And therefore, my opinion of myself was way more important than their opinions. This was the way how I was able to get on top of my emotional, self-inflicted damage.

My biggest dilemma as a teenager was deciding what to do with my life. I wanted a "professional" career, but my dyslexia made reading and writing difficult. This affected the subjects I chose for my final school years.

I was good at athletics, science, and art, so I chose those subjects plus other subjects I had to take. I was one of the strongest kids at school and was part of the relay team, running the 400-meter and 1-kilometer races. I was super fit and often won athletic competitions, but I didn't see sport as a career option for me because of the hereditary diagnosis. I thought, "I could spend years practicing for a sports career, but this diagnosis could come and derail any promising career."

I discovered that it was possible to get into one of the best art colleges in Melbourne with only a Year 11 qualification. I thought I'd have a go. I really wanted to save myself a year by not having to go through Year 12 and the final exams. I was always looking for ways to get out of schoolwork.

I was one of those students who frustrated teachers. "If you just applied yourself, Chris, if you just put the effort in," they'd say, "you'd be a good student and get more than a pass." This was true.

For me it was all or nothing. Anything I showed an interest in, I got an A+. If I wasn't interested, I'd bludge and get the worst results, just good enough to pass. There was no in-between.

There were several ways to get into the art college, and I decided to do the one-off special project. I decided to do an illustration of a kitchen in black and white pencil, a realistic drawing with proper dimensions and perspectives. I locked myself in my room for two full days and immersed myself in my work, only leaving to eat and use the toilet. The finished artwork was very good, so good that even the principal was taken aback. My mum still has the piece hanging in her kitchen to this day. Every time I see the artwork, I remember the two days that I devoted to that project. I remember my hand, my pen, and the thinking around doing the work.

I had to start Year 12 and wait a few days to find out whether I'd gotten into art college. Time stood still. My dad knew I was taking a punt, a long shot, but I knew I had to have a go. I didn't know that I had to check the notice boards at the art college until a friend called me to ask whether I was on the list.

I was learning to drive at the time, so Dad came with me to find out if design would play a role in my future career. He was usually vocal about my driving, telling me to "Slow down" or "Take the corner wider" while holding tight on to his seat belt. Now the silence was nerve-racking. I would have loved him to say something, and he probably should have because I got to the art college in record time.

There were several sheets of paper with lists of names in alphabetical order and "Yes" or "No" next to each.

J for Jankulovski … "Yes."

"Dad, I got in!" I screamed. "Woo-hoo!" We both jumped for joy and embraced each other. We may have even had a dance-off, waving our hands in the air. We were both ecstatic. It felt like I was set for life with a career as a graphic designer.

Getting into college was a bigger deal for Dad than it was for me. It was almost like a lottery win. I could feel the weight of worry shift off his shoulders because he'd been concerned about my future. He often said, "You need a stable job and consistent income; otherwise, you'll have nothing."

My own concerns about how I was going to survive out there in the real world were gone, momentarily. I was young and felt that the world was my oyster. I became one of only four students with a Year 11 qualification to get into the best art college in Melbourne. It was quite an achievement, and it was the first time I had achieved something significant. I don't remember attending a day of Year 12 back at school, but somehow, I managed to get into the Year 12 class photos.

I'd never jumped a year in my life. It really boosted my confidence because it was the first time I'd ever advanced in my education. I made up for the year that I lost during my first grade where they held me back. It made me feel smart, capable of doing something worthwhile. I would call up my friends and ask, "How's school going?" in an almost teasing way. I was having the time of my life. There I was, a suburban kid, going to one of the most prestigious art colleges in the city. I used to be the oldest kid in my class; now I was the youngest.

I was in heaven. For forty hours a week all I had to do was draw and create. No more math, history, and other subjects I hated. Instead, I studied drawing from various eras and different types of design and illustration using a range of media such as pastels, pencils, or paint.

And for the first time in my life, I didn't have to try so hard to pass. I could do just enough to get grades in the 70 percent range, because I knew what had to be done and I enjoyed it. So, while I put in a little effort toward my studies, I took my socializing more seriously. I played a lot of table tennis with my friends and went out enjoying long lunches, partying, and nightclubbing. The college was close to restaurants, shops, cinemas and so many other distractions. I could do anything I wanted. Nothing was mandatory. The girls were super-sexy creative types, and I was mesmerized, like a boy in a candy shop. I was leaning into adulthood, and it was amazing. I loved my life.

Looking back, I have to chuckle. I thought I was putting in enough effort not only to pass but to do reasonably well, at around 70 percent. I didn't know that at that prestigious art college you needed 80 to 90 percent to pass, sometimes even 100 percent. They had high standards.

At the end of my first year at art college, I started to seriously consider the idea of pursuing a design career by going to university. I was really enjoying applying my creativity and wanted to be a graphic designer with a university degree, not just a "finished artist" with a diploma, who would work under a graphic designer. I applied to one of Melbourne's best universities. Friends urged me to apply to all the universities in case I didn't get into this one, but I had my sights set on this one university. To my disappointment, I didn't get in. Although the art college gave me a spot in the finished art class for my second year, I didn't go down that path. And anyway, I was busy and enjoying my new life.

I may have been a bit cocky at the time, but the whole situation was a blessing in disguise because it forced me to question what I was going to do with my life, again. Leaving art college got rid of my safety net. It pushed me out of my comfort zone. If I had stayed, I probably would have made it to university eventually and had a graphic design career, making a nice, cushy income, perhaps owning my own company. At nineteen, it forced me to take a long, hard look at who I truly was and who I wanted to become. I had absolutely no idea.

After leaving college in 1992, my dad asked me, "So what are you going to do now?"

I said, "I don't know."

Dad said, "Well, we've got these boxes that need to be assembled. We've got plenty of work. Do you want to complete some of these boxes yourself for additional income?"

I was fine with this. "Yeah, sure." At least it was a chance to earn money on my own time without having to take a job I didn't like.

I got more work from the factory where my dad worked, but this time the work was a more complex assembly job. We had to drill wire pieces into screws and connect them to other screws within the box. I was paid for a "per-piece" output, not for time worked. ATCO fixed a particular cost for the completion of a particular wiring. Each box would contain 1,200 of these pieces, and they would pay $120 per completed box.

I got my dad to produce an air drill that was like the ones in the factory so I could improve the speed it would take to complete the work—after which I leased a few garages to be used as workspaces for other people I hired to do electrical assembly work. The garages made it easy to deliver and store the finished boxes.

My parents thought I was crazy to get people working for me. Mum was horrified about the responsibility I was taking on, but I had no fear. I liked the idea of coordinating and managing other people. Mum's attitude was, "I'm happy with $6,000 a month." But for me it was, "Wow, the more people I get to work for me, the more money I could make. Why stop at $6,000 a month?"

It was about creating a lifestyle for myself by getting others to do the work. All I had to do was set someone up and leave them to work. I didn't need to repeat the training. It was a one-off effort that would pay dividends for a long time. It was like a cash register—*cha-ching!*—giving me money every month while I did nothing. My dad said to me, "Chris, you've made more in a month than your mom makes almost in an entire year!" This was my introduction to the idea of residual or scalable income.

It's interesting that Mum and people like her perceived what I did as risky. I did rent garages out on a yearly basis (because no one would lease them monthly) but I included one month's notice to exit should something go wrong, so essentially it wasn't a yearly contract. I negotiated terms to suit me. Sometimes I had to exit the lease at eight months, but other contracts lasted the full year or longer.

"Chris, even as a kid you always looked for ways to make money," Mum reflected. I'd proved myself to be very entrepreneurial and good at making money. But I was still craving a career and a sense of meaning and purpose for my life. I didn't have one, and that was still important to me. "What am I going to do with my life?" I asked myself. I still didn't know.

The day of my diagnosis

After a few years of consultations and eye laser treatments, my eye surgeon recommended we find out what was causing the blurry spot in the middle of my vision. He suggested that I get a blood test to find out what was causing my angiomas. I drove myself to a different doctor to discuss the test results. Hopefully, they would show me what was causing the problem with my eye.

That's when I got the awful news. "You have a hereditary condition called Von Hippel-Lindau syndrome." The doctor at the hereditary cancer department at The Royal Children's Hospital Melbourne explained to me that a healthy person has around eighteen thousand DNA strands but I had only twelve thousand. It was a rare condition, he told me. Only one in thirty-six thousand people had it. Today, more is known about VHL. It's a genetic mutation of the DNA strands that causes a lifetime of cysts and tumors, sometimes cancerous, to form in major organs like my brain, kidney, spinal cord, pancreas and so on.

The doctors tested my family members because they suspected one of them may have it. Everyone's tests came back negative from my family. This was surprising to me and made me even more suspicious of the accuracy of their tests and whether I even had VHL.

My diagnosis made a bigger impact on me than I realized. At first, it was denial, but I became more conscious of the time and effort I put into everything because I wasn't sure how long I really had. How do you handle something like this at nineteen? I didn't know how to take it. I wasn't given a booklet or given an explanation about the disease. I didn't have the Internet for research or people to talk to. I didn't know how to respond to this. I was an emotional wreck for two weeks. Before my diagnoses I thought I was invincible and now I am told I would be dead at thirty. I felt robbed of an opportunity in life to find pleasure and have fun. I felt like I was robbed of life itself. All these thoughts came over me. I had no idea how to handle it, so I simply ignored it. It was all so new. I kind of hoped if I could tuck it away, so far away, that it would cease to exist. I was trying my luck. "If I can really ignore it, then maybe it would go away." I put on a brave face and carried on with life pretending like I didn't get that diagnosis. This was the beginning of me running away from my life's problems. It just amplified my inability to make any decisions. I stopped believing in a future. There were so many things that transformed in me that I wasn't even consciously aware at the time.

I told myself life is short and questioned the point of having a career, even though a job in advertising or in some creative outfit was a dream of mine. One reason I never pursued graphic design was that subconsciously I thought, "What's the point? I'm going to be dead by the age of thirty."

Most people live their lives working in a job they hate but find their passions outside of work—they call them hobbies, like fishing or sailing—but I wanted more. It felt as though combining passion with making money was my holy grail. I didn't have time to waste. I wanted my life to count and matter in some way and make money by doing what I loved.

CHAPTER 2

Wild Child

There's only one word to describe me in my early twenties—"cowboy." After my diagnosis of von Hippel-Lindau syndrome, I just didn't care about anyone or anything.

A year after my diagnosis, I quit art college in 1993 when I was twenty. Dad stepped in to help me get my first real job at a lighting factory producing lights for a lighting shop. The only reason I took the job was that I was interested in designing lights. The manager made the job offer more attractive by telling me that if I started at the bottom, working for a year to get to know the whole company process and all its departments, they would groom me for a senior position as a lighting designer. I was willing to pay that price.

I enjoyed driving from the suburbs to the inner city. I liked the idea of doing the work and getting paid for it—"earning" an income for the first time in my life. Even though I was still making money with the boxes business, it was a new experience to feel the rewards of my own labor. With the boxes, it wasn't consistent. The boxes business was only covered when the work was available and when my dad made it available for us. He always made the opportunity for mom, and whenever there was a surplus and they needed a quick turnaround, I was the man they called on.

Another new experience I enjoyed was budgeting. My boxes business did not provide consistent cash because it came in waves when the work was available. Sometimes I'd make huge sums of money from it, and at other times not much at all. But working at the lighting factory gave me a steady income, and I liked being able to budget. I saved every penny I earned. It was easy to spend money that other people earned for me, but with my own hard-earned dollars I was frugal and disciplined.

For ten months at that lighting factory, they stuck me in the metal shop and never moved me. It was soul-destroying. After work, I'd go for a run and then watch television. I didn't see my friends much and I became withdrawn. I was depressed about the job, about my life, about everything.

I remember working at the lighting factory and the early morning starts. In the morning, I would go outside and find a quiet place to drink my coffee. I would watch all the factory workers come in all dressed in their blue uniforms. I knew even back then that I didn't fit in.

For one thing, my mindset was completely different, and I stood out because I was driving a flashy car (a car my father gave me for getting into art school). They were focused on savings, and on working more overtime hours to earn more money. I wasn't thinking about how I could do more overtime. I was questioning a lot. Every time I spoke to other factory workers, it was evident that we weren't thinking the same thing.

I also remember the smell of oil and the constant running of various machines in the background as a steady hum throughout the day. The metal shop was noisy. The metal is cold in your hands and sharp. You have to be very careful not to cut your hands.

One of the workers told me, "My goal is to do this job as long as I can. I want to work here for twenty or thirty years." I was baffled by that. I didn't understand the price people pay for looking after their families and I didn't understand how some men would pay that price to get security for their families. I was just looking at my own desires and thought there is no way I would want to do this for that many years. I thought to myself, "Are you mad?" The factory was cold in the winter, and it was brutal work.

Working at the factory didn't leave me with much of a social life because I was working all the time. When the manager promoted me to foreman of the metal shop, it was a clear sign they were not going to honor their agreement to move me into the design department. So, I quit. Once I quit, I had the time to go back to hanging out with my friends.

While my boxes business funded my lifestyle, I didn't take it seriously. I used the money to pay for golf lessons and rounds, to buy and smoke marijuana and to hang out with my mates. You could say that this whole period of my life was a bit of a blur.

Living with my parents at Greenvale, a typical day for me was finding the energy to wake up, then calling my friends to hang out and get stoned. My friends hung out together all day. Back then, we didn't have cell phones and so you had to start the day together. We'd start with one or two mates getting together, and we'd accrue a few more every hour or so until in the evening we had about fifteen or twenty of us at one place. The front lawn of my friend's house was often littered with cars signaling "party time." And it was— people everywhere, smoking, laughing, being silly and having a good time. We'd move around to different locations as the night went on. Life was one big party. None of us had school, none of us had regular jobs or any type of commitment. Our only ambition was to have fun, have a laugh. I was drinking and partying like a wild child. I didn't care about my health, my future or anything—I assumed I'd be dead by thirty.

I crashed the luxury Holden Calais that Dad had bought me. I was OK, but the car was a total write-off. I bought an old bomb at auction for $500—a canary yellow 1972 Toyota Celica. The radio system I installed was more expensive than the car. I didn't care about this one, and perhaps that reflected my mood at the time—not giving a damn. I used to pile a lot of guys into that car, more than was legal, and we'd smoke dope, play loud music, and ignore speed limits.

The Yellow Canary was unique because something happened to the suspension and the car sort of ... *bent*. It was funny because I practically lived in that car with so many mates piling in and we were always leaning to one side. So, the Yellow Canary became the "bent" car. It must have looked ridiculous, sitting at a fifteen-degree angle, but I could lean against the door comfortably while I was driving, so I left it that way. I liked it.

The whole situation—bent car and bent friends—was hilarious. Well, hilarious at the time. I almost don't recognize my younger self today. We became known around town and known to the cops. It was hard to miss the bent Yellow Canary crammed with pot-smoking twenty-year-olds. If you've seen the movie *Up in Smoke* with Cheech and Chong, we were the suburban version of that.

Whether I was driving with my mates, or driving alone and minding my own business, the cops passing on the other side of the road would turn around and pull me over. We'd throw out our homemade bongs before they got to us.

"Can I have your license, please?" they would ask, or "Can you step out of the vehicle?" They ripped the car apart looking for drugs, checking under the seats or taking the seats out. The cops were getting carried away and ripping things apart that I wondered, "How are we going to put that back?" They didn't do it gently either. They were ripping the car apart with one focus—find the drugs. The cops knew we were stoned; our red-rimmed eyes and uncontrollable laughter gave us away.

We never got caught with anything in the car, but we were always caught in the act of trying to buy drugs or while we were high on marijuana. We knew there were consequences if we got caught, but we didn't care too much about them.

I couldn't even get petrol without the cops hassling me, but I was cool about it. "How's it going?" I'd ask with a big smile. They got to know my first name and even my last name, which is a mouthful for some. I thought, "OK, so what? They'll pull us over, ask us questions, check the car. It might take thirty minutes, no worries." It became routine.

I'd hurry the cop up, blasé about the whole situation. "C'mon mate, I'm running late, I've got somewhere to be." He'd look at me, shaking his head.

I lived the Cheech and Chong lifestyle for a year, getting stoned every day with my old high school friends. It was about having fun and making the most of situations that probably weren't so funny. The daily mission was to find laughter, and we found everything funny when we were stoned, especially the cops.

My parents were freaking out about me because I'd quit my job and was doing nothing. They constantly nagged me, "We worked hard to get you this job. You should work in a job like everyone else. How are you going to earn money? How are you going to live? What's wrong with you? Aren't you normal?"

I was sick and tired of my parents hassling me all the time. So, when one of my friends asked, "Who wants to go to America with me?" I jumped at it.

I was the only one with money, and said, "Yeah, sure. I'll go." Steve had gone to the same school as me but was a few years ahead. He was a huge, 110-kilogram muscly man who worked as a security guard or bouncer on the side. I knew very little else about him.

I just wanted to get away from everyone and everything and have fun. I packed my bags and booked a one-way ticket to good times.

Steve and I came up with a brilliant way to travel on the cheap. We signed up with Auto Driveaway, a car relocation company that employed people—usually tourists like us—to drive vehicles across the States instead of transporting them on semitrailers. I wish I still had those maps from our American road trip today, because we zigzagged the country from Los Angeles to New York and all the states in between.

We'd pick up a car, be told the destination and hit the road. Sometimes we'd get to pick up brand-new cars from car yards, which was a lot of fun. We mostly drove across the southern states, but we did get to Chicago and even Canada. Sometimes we slept in cars. We once had a car stolen when we arrived in LA; other times the car got broken into. Every time something unfortunate would happen, all we needed to do was to report it to the Auto Driveaway so that we were covered.

Steve and I didn't have a travel plan except to score drugs. We didn't know how long we were going to stay in America or where we were going to go. Steve wanted to go to Las Vegas and New York. I was more interested in seeing the world's biggest crater, visiting NASA, or large observatories and exploring nature. At the age of seventeen, I was a member of the Victorian astronomy society. I even built my own telescope. I've always been interested in meteor showers and the universe. I had this fascination when I looked into a telescope, and I would peer into the pitch-blackness to see another world beyond. It brought me out of my own simplicity. It was always mesmerizing to think about there being other planets and universes.

We drove here, there, and everywhere. We drove through cities, suburbs, and deserts. It was amazing. We covered a lot of miles in a short amount of time, saw spectacular sights and found ourselves in crazy situations—mostly because we were young and stupid and always stoned.

One job we had was to drive a brand-new Porsche 944 convertible from Los Angeles to New York in ten days. In LA we stayed in Santa Monica near Venice Beach, and we enjoyed the place and the Porsche so much that we delayed our departure for three weeks, ignoring the company's calls to take the car to its owner.

We were too busy going to parties and searching for pot. We got invited to parties at mansions and to a Hollywood movie director's place. We told everyone, especially the girls, that we'd bought the Porsche for our road trip holiday. The women, especially the cougars, were all over us. Steve was a womanizer and had no trouble converting flirting into sex. I didn't have his level of confidence and covered up my awkwardness by playing hard to get.

After three weeks, we finally felt it was time to head out of LA and head to New York. On the long stretches of driving in the Porsche, Steve and I would listen to music or just enjoy the silence, speeding along, happy and carefree. We both got sore scalps from driving so fast with the top down.

We often didn't see another car for miles. One time when I was doing 137 miles per hour, a car suddenly came out from an intersection in front of us. I slammed on the brakes, crossing over the lines, and passing him on the wrong side of the road at probably half the speed. I almost lost control of the car when I had to swerve. The car skidded at very high speed, and I thought, "Oh my God, I'm going to hit the pole!" We went from this cruising, relaxing state to suddenly heart racing and thinking we were going to die. Thankfully, I got control of the car but in changing gears quickly down from fifth to fourth I blew the clutch.

Steve and I screamed and stuck our fingers up at the country local. We couldn't believe it. He nearly killed us. All he could manage was a dumb-ass, stupid expression on his face.

"No!" I screamed. I let the car glide to a stop. The other car drove past, the driver giving us the finger.

We shook our heads in disbelief with the situation we found ourselves in. "Now what?"

For twenty kilometers behind us and thirty kilometers ahead of us, there was nothing. There was vast open terrain as far as the eye could see. There was nothing. I noticed the silence. I noticed the wind. It was an eerie feeling to be surrounded by nothing in the middle of what felt like nowhere. We stood on the road waiting for another vehicle to stop for us. Every hour or so a truck would pass but not stop. We must have been there for over four hours until finally a truck stopped quite a way up the road. When it stopped, I wondered, "Is it stopping for us? Am I supposed to go to him?" I decided to take off running toward it and left Steve to watch over the car while I cautiously made my way up to the truck.

"Hi, mate. Our car has broken down. Can you take me to the nearest town, please?"

"Sure, c'mon in," said the middle-aged Hispanic man. He wore a cowboy hat and seemed harmless enough. The truck was huge. In order to reach up to the handle, I had to stretch and lift myself up.

We drove and chatted for about an hour when he started telling me about his obese wife and how much he liked her.

I nodded politely.

"I just love having sex with her," the man said, laughing. He described their sex life explicitly and spoke about her in a really demeaning way. Who does that? I'm a stranger and he's a stranger to me. It was creepy. I was stuck in this nutter's truck in the middle of nowhere. My mind went ballistic, wondering where this was going. If he murdered me, no one would ever find me. "So, do you want to meet her?" He gave me a cheeky grin, one tooth missing.

"What do you mean? Now? How? I don't want to go anywhere. I need to get to a town to get the car fixed," I said.

"No, no, no. She's in the back."

With a swipe of his hand, the curtain opened to reveal an entire room that was hidden in the back of the truck. I had no idea it was there. In the middle of the truck bed, there was his obese wife. It was one of the freakiest sights I have ever seen. There was a sky-light in the top of the truck, and the light illuminated the entire scene. She lay on a bed of rubbish at the back of the truck. Her belly rolled over the mattress in folds. She was the fattest person I had ever seen, on a filthy bed, surrounded by empty chip packets, chocolate bars and Coke cans. I was staring right at her. I was in shock. I couldn't say "Hi" or smile. I was stunned at what I was seeing.

"Holy shit," I thought, "they are going to rape me." I'd been desperate for a lift but wasn't expecting this.

"Can you just take me to the nearest town, please?" I mumbled, trying not to look at him or his wife. I couldn't turn my head to look at either of them. I think the driver noticed that I freaked out and decided to stop the truck.

"There's a town over that way called Fruita. You can't see it from here, but it's about two to three miles in that direction." He waved his hand haphazardly, starting to roll a smoke. "Isn't that right, honey?" he shouted to the back of the truck.

"Uh-huh," she replied.

I got out of the kinky truck as fast as I could and watched it disappear into the horizon. The sun was starting to set, and when I looked at the direction the truck driver pointed to, all I could see was rattlesnake country, a Wild West scene with tumbleweeds rolling in the wind. I walked through the foreign landscape, grateful the kinky couple had let me go, but fearful of another deadly sting. Half a kilometer into my walk, I thought, "What if he was lying?" I couldn't see any settlement in the distance—what if there was no town? What sort of name was Fruita anyway? I'd never thought of death so much in a single day. I had no water, food, tent, or any hiking gear. Nothing. But I just kept going.

After a few kilometers, I spotted a small red brick building in the distance. There was nothing else around there. I approached it from the back, and when I turned the corner, I saw a lineup of twenty or more bikers resting against their Harley Davidsons. Some were wearing leather vests, tattoos and all the bikes leaning against the building like what you would see in a TV or movie scene. I froze, and then did something stupid: I pretended to have a gun. I thought that might be a way to say, "Don't mess with me." For a moment I reached for the imaginary gun inside my jacket, then immediately raised my hands up above my shoulders. Some of them jumped up, eyeing me off as if I was a threat. I may have scared them more because I appeared from nowhere—who knows if the behavior saved me from getting into even worse trouble.

"Listen, guys," I said to the biker gang, "I've got a hundred bucks for anyone who can help me get my car from the freeway to a mechanic shop." They all looked like they could potentially kill me, but I didn't feel I had a choice. I didn't even have the hundred bucks on me, as I'd left my wallet in the car.

One of the roughest-looking dudes jumped off his bike and said, "I'll help."

"Is there a Western Union facility in the grocery store inside?" I asked being quick on my feet.

He said there was.

"Give me a minute to organize the money," I said. What a relief.

Inside the grocery store, I desperately asked the checkout lady at the counter if I could borrow a few quarters for an emergency call. Luckily, she gave me some coins and pointed me to a phone on the wall. She must have seen my desperate face and I think she could tell how scared I was. I then called Auto Driveaway to ask for help. They gave me the number of the owner of the Porsche. When his secretary answered my call, I said, "Please tell your boss that I need a hundred bucks right now to get the car towed to a mechanic. I'm in the middle of nowhere. I don't want the car disappearing. We are in a pretty dire situation." She wired me the money via Western Union. Luckily, it all went to plan. I gave the hundred bucks to the biker, and his entire demeanor changed. Suddenly he was smiling and friendly. I found myself on the back of his bike, the first time I had ever ridden on a Harley Davidson and I enjoyed the ride. We headed off to grab a rope and his pickup truck from his house.

We went to his house, and he invited me in. He introduced me to his family. His kid and his wife were hanging out inside, and they were very pleasant. It was a surprising experience coming from the situation I had just been in. We had a moment where we talked, and I explained that I was on a road trip from Australia and the car had broken down on the side of the road. His wife mentioned, "You guys better go because it's getting dark." We almost forgot that we weren't just buddies hanging out. I got carried away telling him about my story.

Finding the Porsche was a challenge because it was dark by this stage and the freeway was two lanes on both carriageways with a wide strip in the middle. Plus, how do you find a black Porsche in pitch-blackness? The biker pulled out a joint, and I was delighted. I was always trying to score marijuana, and here it showed up in the most random time. The biker and I shared a joint, laughing about the situation and I couldn't help wondering how I had got myself into another crazy predicament.

After an hour, we found Steve. We were lucky—the only thing that attracted my attention to the Porsche was a glimmer of the light reflecting on it.

Steve was asleep inside the car and couldn't believe it when I turned up with the biker. Steve immediately noticed our red eyes rimmed from the marijuana, and screamed, "Are you stoned?" When the biker offered him some marijuana he didn't mind so much. We hung around smoking and joking with each other until Steve said, "OK, let's tow this thing."

I remember thinking, "That rope looks super thin. Is it going to hold?" The rope broke as soon as we started towing the Porsche. We'd driven all that way without a suitable rope for towing! "Oh, shit," said our biker acquaintance. He rummaged through his pickup truck and luckily found another rope, but it was short. The journey into Fruita was hairy—only a meter separated the Porsche from the back of the biker's pickup truck. We were stoned and it was dark. It could have been a catastrophe.

We had to stay in Fruita, Colorado, for a few days while the Porsche was being fixed, but finding accommodation was hard because of our ex-criminal, junkie acquaintance. A manager from one local motel, a Ned Flanders lookalike (from *The Simpsons*), pointed his gun at us because he thought we were gangsters. Pretty unnecessary, I thought.

I tried to explain that we were on this grand road trip and visiting from Australia. And instead of just turning us away or telling us they didn't have any vacancies, he just pointed a gun at me. How rude.

I was shocked and angry that he did this instead of just saying, "We're not going to service you. Please leave." Eventually, we found a place to stay and a mechanic to fix the car. After a few days, with a new clutch installed, we were on our way. Unfortunately, just four hours down the road, after filling up the tank at a petrol station just before Denver, the car started behaving strangely. It was early morning and we had to detour to find the nearest mechanic yet again.

We dropped the car off with the mechanic, had lunch nearby and then returned to get the update. The mechanic told us the devastating news: The car had been filled up with dodgy petrol and the fuel pump was busted. It was going to take ten days for the spare parts to arrive. At that point, I'd had enough. We decided to abandon the car.

I called Auto Driveaway and had the mechanic connect with the representative to let them sort out the mess. I'd already wasted time in Fruita and had no intention of staying in Denver. Steve didn't mind staying on, but I made up my mind to leave the very next day. The following morning, I got on a bus to New York. It was the first time Steve and I had parted ways on our six-month American road trip. It was a beautiful and memorable bus journey because the bus took us through a snowy Colorado ski town.

When I arrived in New York I was struggling to find a car before Steve would arrive within a few days. My hope was that our next destination would be Florida. Unfortunately, most of the cars needed to go to LA, where we'd just been. When Steve arrived we started to worry that we might get stuck in New York, paying for our expensive accommodation. The following day or two Auto Driveaway finally offered us a car bound for Phoenix, Arizona. Not what we wanted, but it wasn't LA, so we grabbed it and figured we'd make the most of it exploring the southern parts of the country.

After a very long day on the road, we stopped at Dallas for a few days and then made our way to New Mexico where we came across a huge store selling fireworks. They're legal in New Mexico, and we went shopping in this store with the widest range of fireworks we'd ever seen. I grabbed the biggest trolley and filled it. We drove until dark, and I made Steve pull over so I could light a few fireworks. First, we got stoned, of course. We lit big and small fireworks and produced a spectacular show—not realizing we'd pulled over right across from the biggest police compound in New Mexico.

Two police cars were on their way over. "Oh shit!" we both said, and quickly hid the marijuana in the bushes. I lit up a few more fireworks before they arrived.

"You're in a bit of trouble, boys. You can't light up fireworks beside the highway. Do not light anymore," one of the police officers warned us. I didn't want them to go to waste, and the display had taken me forever to prepare, so despite his warning, I intentionally continued to light a few more fireworks in front of him.

He was so mad that he almost hit me and began to confiscate the lot.

"What? Oh, no way, man! This is my dream; you can't take my fireworks," I begged and started apologizing, doing everything I could to keep my fireworks. Eventually, the police officer agreed that I could keep some of them on the condition that we would leave New Mexico right away.

We couldn't believe he followed us all the way. When we finally crossed the border into Arizona, the policeman turned around. We immediately pulled over to the side of the road to get a few hours of sleep.

In the morning we made our way to the Grand Canyon. We parked at the Grand Canyon and later that night decided to light up the rest of the fireworks. Drunk as skunks, we saved the "monster" until last. It was four inches wide, a fat rocket and one of my most expensive ones. It came in a kit with instructions about how to stand, position and launch it.

I modified the holding bracket of the rocket so it would fire horizontally into the canyon rather than straight up in the sky. When I lit it, it exploded with such force that the ground shook and the sound echoed through the canyon. It ricocheted, and unfortunately hit the metal railings of the viewing platform and instead of going out into the void, it fired down into the canyon, hitting a dry tree, and setting it ablaze. We started a fire in the Grand Canyon and had to make a run for it. Luckily it was just a bush and not much else.

We heard sirens from the park rangers' cars. We packed our gear quickly and ran, again. With the rangers on our tails and Steve on the wheel, I let off smoke bombs to block their path. We found the whole situation hilarious.

I looked back and shook my head. I couldn't believe we did all that. In America, I thought I was immune from the law, or above it, because I was a tourist. Nowadays there's no way you can behave so stupidly.

After five months of journeying throughout the States, Steve and I parted ways again and traveled to Europe independently.

A few weeks later, we met up again in Florence, Italy. After our wild adventures in the United States, I didn't expect to get into anything crazy in Europe. But it seemed like my run-ins with the law weren't quite over.

Since Florence was famous for its leather, Steve wanted to buy a leather jacket. We went to a street market that was packed with people. We enjoyed the shopping because we found stall after stall of leather vendors along the narrow laneways.

Steve was a muscly 110-kilogram guy, and he had trouble finding a leather jacket that fit him. Being an Australian man of Italian descent, and wearing that leather jacket, he looked pretty mean.

As we continued our shopping, buying a few other things along the way, we heard a police siren in the background. We were surprised to see a car driving down this extremely tight and busy street full of people, crawling its way through the crowd.

We were at a kiosk in the middle of the laneway as the car came closer. We turned around and tried to get out of the way for the car to pass.

Instead, the car stopped in front of us, and two policemen stared at us from inside the car. We turned around to see if they were looking at someone else. We were surprised that they were looking directly at us, and suddenly we noticed everybody else was also looking at us.

The policemen signaled for us to get in the car as it was pretty noisy in the market. In broken English, they said we had to go to the police station.

"There must be a mistake. What's going on? We've just arrived in Florence."

"We explain at police station," said a police officer.

We thought we'd go along with them for the ride. After all, we didn't have much of a choice.

The policemen were very casual and playful in the car. I remember how these guys took the opportunity to race on the tight, winding streets of Florence. We felt like we were on a racetrack. The policeman was driving the car with sirens blaring. It was such a full-on, incredible experience.

I remember the car hitting an old lady's shopping bag and scattering her things everywhere. That was how aggressive the policeman's driving was. They drove so fast, with pedestrians and cars on either side, and we hung on for dear life. They even used the handbrake to make turns through sharp corners. I felt like I needed a harness.

We were enjoying the ride, laughing with the policemen and they were laughing with us. We were in the moment. It was a casual scenario.

The car raced along a narrow street when suddenly, the driver slammed on his brakes, yanked his handbrake up to turn into the tight driveway of a reasonably sized compound. We found ourselves at a police station.

As we all got out of the small Alfa Romeo police car, I noticed how tall the policemen were. They looked like giants. Suddenly, their demeanor went from casual to seriously pissed. They started talking in Italian. There was a dramatic change in their attitude toward us. One moment we were having fun with them during this amazing ride, the next thing we knew, they were angry with us. We were confused.

Even though Steve was of Italian descent, he didn't fully understand what was going on. The policemen were talking very fast.

We were put in individual cells, temporary holding spots with a metal bench to sit on. I just sat there concerned because I didn't know what was going on. Steve and I hadn't done any drugs at all, it was our first day in Florence.

"Hey, I want to call the Australian embassy. What you guys are doing is criminal," I complained loudly. "Tell us what we've done?"

They didn't tell us anything for about an hour. Then they moved me from my cell into another room where I had to speak to a different officer who wore a suit. I didn't know who he was. He looked like an investigator or detective. He was asking a lot of questions in Italian and his English was so broken I could barely understand him. I remembered he had a stick and slapped it on the table. I was really scared he was going to hit me with it.

It was during that interrogation that I began to understand what the allegation was. The police thought Steve was a mafia person involved in some recent scam to do with printing money. When he bought the jacket, Steve received a lot of change in counterfeit lira. We just landed in the country and couldn't tell the difference between real and counterfeit lira. It was obvious to the locals, though, and that's why we were reported straight away.

We were accused of printing the money and having more of it. They talked to me in Italian because they thought I was an Italian pretending to be Australian. The interrogation went on for hours. I was getting hungry and exhausted.

Finally, the police let us go later in the afternoon. Before they released us, they took our watches, wallets, and even our hotel keys. They didn't return any of it. We expected a lift back to our hotel. Instead, they escorted us out onto the street and shut the large iron gates of the police compound leaving us on the street to figure out how to get back to our hotel without any money or any idea where we were. We were completely lost and disoriented. I don't recall how but eventually we managed to find our way back to our hotel.

When I share these stories with friends today, they can't believe I did all that. Neither can I!

My wife looks at me in shock because she's never seen me drunk or stoned. Now approaching fifty, I look back, shake my head and smile. Our travel adventure was like a comedy movie, and there were plenty of other crazy situations where Steve and I brushed with death or narrowly escaped serious injury. The characters we played then grew up—thank God.

CHAPTER 3

Black Sheep to Self-Made Man

Home, sweet home. It was good to be back in Australia. I was at Sorrento Beach, just outside Melbourne. My friends and I wanted to catch up and have a weekend trip away. Ten of us got together to catch up with me and swap stories of our adventures. So we rented a holiday house. Kids were making sandcastles; people were sunbathing, swimming, and surfing. Just your usual day at an Aussie beach.

I went bodysurfing, and I was catching the waves, lost in the moment. I looked behind me and noticed I was five hundred meters from shore and being carried away by a strong riptide.

I tried desperately to swim back but I was fighting against the rip, and by the time I swam halfway toward where the big waves began, I was exhausted. I got stuck at the break, and as I surfaced, another massive wave heaved over me. Then another, and another. I was stuck in a rapid set of waves and couldn't hold my breath any longer. I went under and inhaled water.

With water in my lungs and the waves tossing me every which way, I felt an overwhelming sense of peace. My life flashed like a movie playing in front of me, starting with me then and there, at twenty-one, drowning. I saw my family and friends, events big and small came and went, taking me back through the years to when I was very young. Despite all this, I knew I wasn't going to give in and fought to get out of it. I was fighting for my life.

One of the big waves disoriented me, and I lost my sense of direction. Inadvertently, as I swam away from the shore, I found myself getting out of the rip. It was chaotic, a blur, but slowly, I realized I was making my way back toward the shore. Before long I found myself on the shore, heaving on all fours with water pouring out of my mouth, feeling as if I was going to faint at any minute, I could barely see. Everything was so bright. Two lifeguards approached me out of nowhere and asked, "Do you need help?" I mumbled, "No, where were you when I needed you most? I was drowning."

Just another day at the beach turned out to be another near-death experience for me. Afterward, my mates and I had a few drinks back at the house, joking about what had been a very serious situation.

Could you imagine sharing all these stories and then adding to them in the moment? The first night I was talking about my crazy American and European adventures with Steve and then the following day I'm talking about my most recent up-to-the-minute near-death experience and we're having a laugh about that.

But once I was back home, it was hard adjusting back to ordinary life after all that traveling. I felt depressed. Steve and I had done such crazy stuff in America and Europe that home was dull by comparison. The same question plagued me as before I left: "Chris, what are you going to do with your life now?" I still had no idea.

I thought working in the advertising industry would be something I like to do. Its creative energy and the buzz of sales and marketing intrigued me. I was envious of the people I saw working in advertising—they were well paid, well-dressed, going out to lunch and working in creative environments. The lifestyle seemed cool and I wanted that. I applied for numerous jobs within the industry, but only managed to get one interview for a sales position selling cinema advertising on a commission basis. I thought that was rubbish and declined the offer.

I even offered my services to advertising agencies for free. A graphic designer friend was going to an advertising awards night in Melbourne, and she asked me to join her. I thought this was potentially a great way into the industry. I had business cards printed, saying: "My DNA is built for advertising, and I'd like to prove it by working for free for a week or two." Throughout the evening I placed cards on every table. At the end of the night, most of them were still lying around. Weeks went by and nobody took me up on that offer. Not being able to get in and live that "romantic" notion of a career in advertising was a big letdown. I was at a loss. I felt I'd run out of options, with all doors slammed in my face.

For the first time in my life, I started seriously worrying about my future. I couldn't understand why no one was giving me a chance, even though I was willing to work hard and prove myself.

I became an angry young man and started going out a lot, drinking, partying, and hanging out with a bunch of nightclub friends. I didn't know who they were, which school they had been to or where they lived. I never saw them in the daylight. I had a lot of fun with these nocturnal party-animal friends, but they weren't real friends like my old schoolmates.

After a few months living back at home, Mum and Dad were nagging me about my life yet again. "Get up. Get out of bed. Get a job. Do this, do that." It drove me crazy, and to be honest, I'd had enough of just hanging out and doing nothing all day.

A few months after I returned from my travels and adventures, Dad intervened again and organized an interview for me at ATCO, the company he worked for, but this time for something more interesting.

During the interview, the manager couldn't decide whether to put me into his marketing or production management team. Then he opened a chess board and said, "OK, if you beat me at chess, I'll put you into management." Dad must have mentioned that I was a good chess player.

It was an unusual interview approach, but I went along with it. We had a good game, with long silent pauses, until I proclaimed, "Checkmate!"

He gave me the role of production manager in charge of sixty staff. Even though Dad couldn't read or write English well, his people-management skills were superb. I think the boss wanted to see if I also had good management skills. It was a lot to live up to.

I wasn't managing people but the flow of production. I worked in the copper mill division, where large spools of copper were reduced to various thicknesses and grades to be used for transformers. I enjoyed scooting around in the forklift, organizing everything. I maneuvered the finished items and had them weighed and measured before depositing them into a large holding bay, where the warehouse team would put them into storage. I had to prepare the feed machines, take inventory of the stock, and make sure that the right people were in place to operate the machines.

After two and a half years at ATCO, I was bored. I woke up to the alarm, went to work, did mind-numbing, repetitive work, came home, had dinner, watched TV, and went to bed. Every day was "Groundhog Day." The life was being squeezed out of me again.

Working at the factory gave me insight into why my dad enjoyed his job as a production manager. His job was to make sure that the overall production flowed smoothly and to generally increase the volume and speed of operations, which are all very much dependent on the people operating the machines. As the person responsible for hiring these people and being the people person that he is, he had to make sure that he was helping the staff succeed in the role in order to reach the company production goals. Mr. Gjergja, his boss, was his good friend and valued him as an employee. I could see that the boss drove flashy cars and had money, big money that all the employees and my dad helped him accumulate.

I couldn't believe my dad loved his job; I couldn't do the job over the long term like he did. When I looked at Dad, I knew what I didn't want to be. That may sound harsh, but it was true at the time, regarding work, taking risks and creating a big business. When I wanted to invest in something, Dad's response was, "Don't invest in that. It's a waste of money." When I wanted to buy something, he said, "Don't buy that." All I heard was, "Don't take the risk."

Don't. Don't. Don't.

I got sick of listening to his fear and being told what to do. I began to hate my father.

I was furious when my Dad intervened in a property purchase I tried to make in 1997. In downtown Melbourne there was an old building that was the first of its kind to be converted into a residential apartment building and I went to see it. I was curious. I wanted to see what they had done in terms of refurbishing this place. I loved the unusual architecture and the location. It was close to my favorite clubs and party spots. I thought, "Hey, this is cool. I like it; I want to buy it." I left a deposit, but the next day, my Dad begged the agent to give me a refund within the two- to three-day cooling-off period.

The agent refunded my deposit and the sale did not proceed. A year later the property market in Melbourne boomed and the value of that property I attempted to purchase had doubled from $250,000 to $500,000. I could have used the equity to invest in more properties. I could have created wealth with property by investing much earlier in my life. The irony is that Dad was so fearful about my financial situation that inadvertently his actions put a stop to my first investment and derailed any career I might have been able to carve out as a property investor. At a minimum, I could have owned a fully paid-off apartment.

But imagine if I did make that money, I would have been game to buy more property and to take on more risk as the market was booming. This was the first opportunity presented to me to create wealth and get out of this trap of trying to figure out what to do with my life. You think a moment like that is once in a lifetime and will never manifest again.

Mum and I still talk about this. "I can't believe what your father did all those years ago," she says, shaking her head in disappointment. It just goes to show, though, that even though you may miss one big opportunity in life, others can follow, more doors will open. I'm proof of that.

Dad made it clear he didn't approve of me and our relationship really soured. I lost confidence in him. I even gave up cigarettes because he smoked; I didn't want any association with him.

I was so sick of Dad nagging me and imposing his views on me that I had to get out. What's more, I didn't want to be spending my days in a boring job for a middling wage.

"I'd rather be broke than live on my knees for you or for anyone," I told him.

"I got you this job. How can you quit? You need security!" he screamed. "How will you live? What's wrong with you?"

At twenty-four, I came to terms with my inability to find a job that I would enjoy doing. So, I quit the last job I would ever have as an employee. I quit the idea of having other people control how much I could earn or opportunities I could have. I asked myself, does society genuinely expect me to work hard at a job I don't like for the next forty years, earning an income that can barely pay the bills? Do I have to settle for this?

I moved out of my parents' home into my own apartment. It was only twenty minutes away from the family, but it gave me enough breathing space to allow my high-energy personality and entrepreneurial zeal to flourish.

I moved to an inner Melbourne suburb called South Yarra. My apartment was near Chapel Street—an upscale shopping area. I made the most of the café culture, restaurants, and nightclub life-style in the area. I also found myself a girlfriend. We had a really good time and partied hard. I called Dad every few weeks, but that's as far as it went. I wouldn't visit. Mum and I had a turbulent relationship too. She had a strong Macedonian accent and couldn't speak English well, so I was closer to Dad. Don't get me wrong, she was my mother, but at the time I felt indifferent toward my family. Their attitude influenced my beliefs and values, but in a negative way—I reacted against them. My father's life was an example of how I didn't want to live my life. I wanted the life of his boss—driving the flashy car and owning a big business.

I started a process of self-directed learning, unlearning a lot of the conditioning I'd received from my family. I had to let go of my father's views and fears. They were his beliefs, not mine. I saw clearly how hanging on to disempowering worldviews kept people stuck in their comfort zones. I questioned all my beliefs and assumptions, searching for new perspectives and ways to live my life.

Then I forced myself to learn to read. At school I'd never read a book, not one. I actually paid a lot of attention in class, because my learning difficulty made me find alternative ways of obtaining information. I was cunning enough to learn from conversations, from storytelling, from listening and asking a lot of questions—a skill that has helped me as an entrepreneur.

I instinctively knew that education via self-directed learning was the only way out of my current circumstances. Previously I'd felt formal education was something you had to do to get a piece of paper that got you a good job. As a teenager, I hated formal education. I couldn't excel in it and felt my life might be doomed without having a degree. But as a young adult, I came to understand how important education really was—without the schooling structure.

I read everything I could get my hands on, a vast range of things that interested me—books on psychology, business, marketing and how to make money. I even read the whole Bible with supplementary books. All day, every day, I stayed home and read. I underlined important information, studied, took notes, and reflected on what I had learned. I spent thousands of dollars buying courses or attending courses, and it was nothing for me to invest $10,000 here or $5,000 there. I was investing in myself, in my education and my future.

I read close to nine hundred books. That's all I did for the better part of a year from the time I woke up to the time I went to sleep. Believe it or not, the first book I ever read in full was at the age of twenty-four. I just couldn't believe I woke up to this, to books. I was awakened to different thinking and ideas and I found myself questioning things and understanding things in a different way with my new information. I was like a sponge; I was so hungry. If I fell in love with a topic I would read ten to thirty other books on the topics in the genre.

I needed to take stock of my life, to determine where I was, where I wanted to be and how to get there. But first I had to identify my goals. I didn't know what I wanted to do, but I did care about having a satisfying, meaningful career.

I always visualized myself as a wealthy businessman but, I was nowhere near that. I wanted to get out of the fantasy trap I was stuck in and take action. I had to take it step by step. You can't run before you crawl, right? That was a big lesson for me: realizing that I couldn't skip one hundred steps to get to the top. I had to take a step, see where that would lead me and then take another step, always knowing that I was moving forward, closer to my goal. I was excited for the first time in ages, realizing that by applying myself and learning from my experiences, I could make substantial progress with small steps even if there were failures along the way.

I gave up on the idea of a career in advertising, or any industry. I was going to focus on becoming an entrepreneur (even though I already was one with my boxes business). As an entrepreneur I could be as creative as I wanted to be.

I paid thousands of dollars for advice from consultants and did personality tests to figure out what I was best suited to. I was constantly looking for answers, searching outside myself.

Then I had another "aha" moment. I questioned why I was always looking for answers outside of myself. What the hell was I doing? Those consultants knew less about some things than I did. To live a truer and more authentic life, I had to start believing in myself.

I had so many revelations during my self-education process, but none more important than the idea of decision-making and action-taking. None of my self-education mattered unless I was prepared to make a decision and apply myself.

In fact, I rejected the idea of studying anything related to a long-term future—my short life expectancy was always on my mind. My VHL condition made the long term irrelevant, so what was the point in studying for a future I might not have?

From the experience of applying what I learned, I developed more discernment and better judgement, significantly improving my decision-making. I was able to make better decisions faster and more accurately on all types of things. For me, this was a true education.

I decided that I was going to be a go-getter, a mover and shaker. I would assess situations and be prepared, but I believed that taking action and being adaptive to change was more important than mapping out a whole overarching plan.

At first, I was afraid of taking this approach. Mindful of my lack of a formal education and career path, all I could see was me hitting the ground with a thud. But it became apparent that I just needed to take a leap of faith. The moment I started believing in my own capacities, I learned that I could not only fly but really soar and live the life I wanted.

I was ready to learn on the fly.

In my search to become an entrepreneur, I learned that the most important thing about business was value: the ability to add value, to sell that value, to market that value and to put people together to deliver on that value. I practiced all these things when I established my first business.

I was still assembling boxes for ATCO at this time, but I started to take the idea of assembling more seriously. I created a new company to provide on-demand staffing solutions for large factories around my area to do with packaging and assembling. I called it Industry Outplacement.

I wrote a letter—which contained many spelling mistakes—and put my mother's phone number down as the contact number. I sent the letter to one thousand of the largest manufacturers around the greater Melbourne area. The following day I went to my parents' home to tell Mum that I'd just done some marketing for a new business idea and used her number as I hadn't yet registered a phone line at my new apartment. I asked her, "If anybody calls, please get their first name and contact details so I can call them back."

The first prospective client who called got a surprise when Mum answered in her strong Macedonian accent.

"Who this is?"

When I got on the phone, the guy asked, "Is this a real business?"

"Yes, of course. How can I help?"

He asked me to come and do a quote for an emergency job he had. A shipment of millions of gloves had just arrived from China. The packaging on all of them had the wrong barcode, and he wanted a quote to put stickers of a new barcode over the old barcode urgently. He contacted me because he didn't have an on-demand workforce, which was what I advertised (but didn't have, by the way).

I showed up at my prospective client's factory and offered a quote that was incorrect. I'd computed every minute as one hundred seconds, not sixty, so my quote came in ridiculously cheap. The client was impressed with my solution to add the stickers. Everyone else had said they had to undo the packaging, which made it difficult to put the gloves back in their original sleeve that contained twelve gloves. I'd figured out a way to add the stickers without fully removing the gloves from the packaging so that we could finish the job faster than anybody else.

The client sensed that I was a bit of a cowboy but was willing to take a chance on me.

"Deliver on time and price, OK?"

I checked my quote but still couldn't see my mistake. He called again, asking for reassurance. "Please double-check your numbers. I have the trucks coming to your warehouse tomorrow."

I was worried that I'd made a mistake with my quote and a friend confirmed that I had indeed computed every minute incorrectly. This was clearly the problem my client was alluding to.

Oh no! I had made a big mistake. But when I called the client, he was so desperate that he said, "I thought so. Don't worry—just send me the new quote and get on with the job. I'll pay you whatever when you're finished."

I was so relieved. The massive weight on my shoulders became a celebration. I was basically given an open checkbook to get a job done for the duration of the six weeks of work. I applied myself without any financial limitations for the first time in my life. I was holding my breath, as I didn't know how it was going to turn out. I hired a team of twenty-five people and delivered the job faster than any of us had anticipated.

My forklift, warehouse and equipment rental suppliers all recognized me as a desperate young man trying my luck in business for the first time.

With that first business endeavor serving an Australian cleaning products company, I made in just six weeks what I'd previously made in a year. It was a major moment in my life—It made me think about the perception of money and how we were brought up with the thinking that you need a job for security, but money doesn't work that way, it's not linear. It was the first time in my life that I witnessed and experienced leverage like that. It was incredible to think that I didn't have to be stuck on a pay grade. This notion of earning money, crazy money, without a job was mind-boggling for me. I resolved that I'd build a career as an entrepreneur, and deal with the inevitable mistakes and failures along the way. That job set the stage for the entrepreneurial journey I'm still enjoying more than twenty years later. I am delighted that I've persevered.

My business grew quickly from that point. My second client was ATCO, which gave me a higher volume of work when I went into business for myself, with Remington and three other large manufacturing companies joining soon after.

I was making money, but I was soon bored. I thought money equated to success, but I wasn't happy, and to me that meant failure.

I thought I was doing all the right things to be happy—starting a business I was familiar with, had experience in and was able to expand. I played to my strengths, which was creating value, attracting clients and marketing. However, making all this money and simply coordinating just wasn't satisfying enough. I was craving an outlet for my creativity and still searching for something that would fuel my soul, give me purpose, and enable me to contribute in a more meaningful way.

While I was in the process of searching for a product to manufacture and sell, a friend invited me to an event, which was my introduction to the network marketing company Amway. It was exciting, the products were good, and the people were pumped. These were the sort of people I wanted to be associated with. I immersed myself in the Amway business, in addition to working in my Industry Outplacement business.

I know that Amway now has a bad reputation and I know people have had bad or unfortunate experiences or issues with the tactics and whatnot, but I had a great experience. I enjoyed the people who want to personally grow as individuals, and who want to earn money for themselves. I was engaged in personal development at that time, and I loved the fact that I had the opportunity to refine my sales skills and meet people.

A lot of the people in Amway were born-again Christians and often socialized together, so I went along to barbeques, picnics, and church. Most of the people in this community were young. During church activities, there was much music and dancing and celebration in recognition of the higher power of love. While I didn't really sing and dance, I enjoyed the atmosphere. I'm aware of the Holy Spirit and I felt its presence many times as I immersed myself in these celebrations.

The Christian community in Amway was a huge influence on me, and it was the beginning of my own personal spiritual journey. I rented a houseboat three hours from Melbourne at Lake Eildon and spent two weeks alone there. At twenty-six years of age, I allowed God into my life and became a born-again Christian.

I've heard someone say that being spiritual is like living your life on a tire that's full. It's enriching. You acquire powerful traits and qualities to live by, along with a community that speaks your language and shares your point of view. But it's just a point of view. As much as I enjoy Christianity, I wanted to step back and learn about other religions as well. I've since taken whatever philosophies, stories and ways resonated with me from the other major faiths like Buddhism and Hinduism, but I practice mindfulness more than anything else in my life.

I certainly have faith. How can I not have faith? I've been on Christian and Buddhist pilgrimages and studied the Bible and other books on spirituality. It's one of my major interests besides sales and marketing, business, and wealth creation. I always work from a perspective of love and spirituality, as it always gets the best results.

After a year of strenuous effort trying to grow my multilevel marketing business, I wasn't having much success from marketing Amway. I loved the people and the community, but I could see that I was having more success with Industry Outplacement than most people who were trying to build a multilevel marketing business within Amway, so I left and continued my learning at my pace.

One afternoon in 1998, I saw a TV program on life coaching as a new career. I sat up, interested, and thought, I wouldn't mind doing that. It looked like a great opportunity to make money and do work that was more fulfilling by helping others achieve their goals.

After the show, the phone rang. It was a friend who said, "I just saw this awesome show on TV and thought of you." Not long after, I got a call from another friend, who also urged me to investigate life coaching. I thought, OK, God, I don't need any more clues. On that day, I decided to become a life coach, just like that.

I created a one-page promotional flyer with a blurb about who I was, offering a six-month coaching program. I made it enticing by offering the first month for free and priced the program at $750 a month with fortnightly sessions at forty-five minutes per session. I thought that putting myself out there as a life coach was worth having a shot so that I could get immediate feedback.

That afternoon, I went to a property investment seminar being held nearby, stood at the entrance, and handed out my flyer as people came in. Nobody knew that I was not part of that event, but I could see people wondering who this guy was, handing out the flyers. The moment somebody realized I wasn't supposed to be doing it, I ran. I didn't think anyone would call me, but to my shock nineteen people contacted me the following day. Holy cow!

People from all walks of life wanted to meet with me. There were businesspeople, a doctor, people wanting to start a business, and people wanting something more out of life. I'd meet them at a coffee shop for a face-to-face chat. I really had no idea what I was doing, but it was refreshing to observe the challenges of others rather than my own.

I asked them all what they wanted to accomplish within the six months, and what they wanted to achieve in their lives. I thought about who I felt comfortable working with and out of the nineteen people, I chose thirteen to coach. I went from earning no money to being a life coach with the capacity to earn almost $10,000 a month for the next five months.

"We've had an overwhelming response, so we'll start in two weeks," I told them all. In fact, I was trying to buy time so that I could learn about life coaching. I bought as many books on it as I could and devised a curriculum myself.

As I learned about my clients and what they wanted to achieve, I customized my material and tailored my solutions to their needs. Whatever their next step or goal was, I read up on it, and offered insights from the books I'd read, for them to apply immediately. I practiced my self-directed learning techniques on my clients, and it worked.

After the first month's free trial, no one dropped out. I was nervous about it, but they were all happy to continue with my coaching. Over six months, everyone made steady, sound progress with their goals except for one woman who achieved spectacular success by wildly exceeding some of hers. While I was happy for her, I hadn't achieved that same level of success. I realized I needed to listen to my own advice first.

It was around this time, when I was twenty-five, that my eyes started to cause me grief again. I developed internal scarring due to all the previous laser treatments on my eye. I had to have an operation to suck up all the black fluid that was causing floaters in my eye and drain it away from the scar tissue.

During the operation, I experienced the ultimate nightmare, yep, I woke up in the operating room just as the doctor was about to start the procedure. I remember a needle sliding on the surface of my eye. My jaw was clamped so I couldn't say anything except make "*Mmm, mmm*" noises. I was freaking out. I was conscious of everything the doctors were saying and could even hear the radio in the background. When the doctors realized something was wrong, they must have increased the dosage of the anesthetic.

After the operation, I was moved to an intensive care ward of some sort. I remember sitting upright on the bed. Then I heard the heart-monitoring machine flatline, making a loud continuous beep. I looked down just in case the monitoring device on my finger had come off, but it was still there. I remember being fully conscious during this time. I saw the doctors and nurses running toward me, telling me to breathe. Everything around me gradually went white and completely silent. It was as if time had slowed down. I felt peaceful and relaxed. I was aware of the things happening around me, but there was an invisible wall that separated me from everything else. It was like an out-of-body experience. I remember thinking to myself, "Hey, I'm not going anywhere.

My sister's getting married soon." Then I snapped back into consciousness, surrounded by nurses trying desperately to bring me back to life.

This experience was another example of my theory that during these near-death events, you experience time in a different dimension. You're also given a choice whether you want to continue to live or to die.

I chose life each time.

CHAPTER 4

Reinventing Myself

On the surface, I was a success. My company Industry Outplacement was profitable, but I was still searching for meaningful work. I was grateful that my company bought me time so that I could focus on my self-directed learning and grow as a person, but I wanted more.

In 2000, I kept operating Industry Outplacement, but I was exploring simple product ideas with a view to commercializing them and establishing new distribution channels. Once I had distributors on my side, I knew I could build a business by continuing to make new products into the future. I thought, how nice would it be to design something and let it sit on someone else's shelf selling itself automatically? I wouldn't need to worry about a team, or all the problems associated with managing people, but could just focus on finding the right distributor for my products.

I decided to commercialize one of my product ideas I named Easylog—a little gadget that prompted you to record manually how many kilometers you drove for business or private use. Every time you started your car, a voice-recorded message would say, "Record your vehicle logbook journey now." It was a novelty product to complement the sale of vehicle logbooks.

I calculated that 1.5 million logbooks were sold in Australia every year and I thought if I could make a dollar from every one of those, I could easily triple my money. I thought it would be that easy. Another rookie mistake. I believed that millions of people would buy my branded vehicle logbooks over its competitors because it was combined with this reminder gadget and sold for just a few dollars more. The other logbooks were boring, administrative types, but mine was interesting, fun, and packaged better.

Eventually, I managed to book a meeting with a buyer working with the largest stationery supply chain in Australia. He urged me to set my sights overseas after I had shown him the quotes I got from my local manufacturer. He advised me it would be way cheaper to manufacture the product in China and said the cost to produce the gadget in Australia would make it too expensive for consumers. "If you can produce the product for under a few dollars, not including the logbook, I'll order twenty thousand units from you," he told me.

I made a few modifications to a purchasing contract my lawyer had prepared a few weeks before the meeting. The distributor signed it right there and then. Next, I went to see my dad to tell him I had gotten a deal. He was a little surprised, but he was used to my business ideas by this point. I asked him if he was willing to fund 80 percent of the production for this gadget. He thought about it for a few moments, asked me a few questions, then said, "Chris, are you sure you know what you're doing?"

"Not 100 percent sure, but given the large order, I am sure I could make it happen." I then asked Dad if he knew of any suppliers in China that could help me make my product.

He said there was a supplier in Taiwan who produced electronic things. With contract in hand, I hopped on a plane to Taiwan to meet this supplier, a man named Eddy. I'd never been to Taiwan and was super excited.

Eddy picked me up at the airport in Taipei. He told me he thought it was a good idea to meet with some other suppliers while I was there and get quotes from them, too. I felt comfortable with him straightaway, and said to him, "Actually, if you could produce my product for a price similar to these other suppliers, I'd love for you to do it." I asked him to make thirty thousand units, adding ten thousand to the order the distributor had made, just to be sure I would have enough product.

He agreed on one condition: "Before we do business, we have to become friends first."

To celebrate our deal, Eddy took me to a special restaurant for dinner. He asked me questions about having my products manufactured and about my business experiences generally. I shared a story about my father and the factory he worked at and told him about my Industry Outplacement business. After dinner, Eddy introduced me to some of his work colleagues and we all went to a karaoke bar.

We sat at a private table and the girls who were serving brought us bottles of whiskey and little cups. They poured us shots and shouted, "*Gan bei*" (Taiwanese for "cheers"). Some of Eddy's colleagues started singing and dancing with the girls. It was the first time I had experienced something like this, and I was having a great time. It was cool, but it was also the kind of place you didn't want to be seen in.

We continued drinking, finishing one bottle after another. The next thing I knew I was up singing as well. Then it all hit me. The room started spinning and I was about to throw up. I ran to the toilet and got there just in time. One of the girls came with me, but then she started throwing up as well after watching me puke. Poor girl.

When we emerged, Eddy suggested it was time to drop me off at my hotel. But when we arrived, I started throwing up again. Eddy waited outside my hotel room, listening through the door, very worried about me. I could barely talk, but I managed to say, "Mate, I've never thrown up like this in my life."

Eddy said, "Chris, let me take you to the hospital. I think you need to get checked."

The next thing I knew, we were at a Taiwanese hospital. I was the only foreigner there. Fortunately, the doctor spoke English. After checking me, he told me I had alcohol poisoning. It was the first and only time that has happened. After the doctor treated me, I started feeling a bit better and Eddy went home to get some sleep. The hospital called a taxi to take me back to my hotel.

A few days later, I reconnected with Eddy and said, "I'm better now—thank you very much for the experience!"

Eddy put a contract together and as I was reading it, I looked at him and shook my head. I couldn't understand anything in it. It was in English, but, maybe because I'm dyslexic, I couldn't quite figure out what it said. So instead, I asked him questions like, "Can you produce this much? Can you produce the products within six weeks? Can you deliver all the way to the port in Australia?"

Once Eddy had answered all my questions and put my mind at rest, I signed the contract. I gave him a 50 percent deposit and told him I would pay the rest once I received photos of the products being shipped to Australia.

And then the unthinkable happened. Weeks away from the arrival of the products, the supplier who had ordered twenty thousand units canceled his order. What's worse, my contact at the supplier got fired, making it even more challenging to sort out the problem. And all of this happened within weeks of me paying my manufacturer in full.

I was struggling. I ended up storing the items at a warehouse. Then I spoke to the person who replaced the buyer working with the large supplier. I explained what had happened, and he advised me to connect with a competitor of mine that also published logbooks and a variety of other stationery products.

This competitor had fourteen other products and a long history as a supplier to this stationery chain, whereas I was an independent innovator with just one new product. My competitor was only interested in my gadget to boost the sale of its own boring vehicle logbook but combining my gadget with a boring administrative logbook was a doomed idea. As a result, my gadget never really got the exposure it needed to succeed.

I had to fly frequently to Sydney to work with my competitor to get the Easylog out on the shelves. It quickly became clear that my competitor and the stationery chain had no interest in producing a large new order.

I terminated my "partnership" with both and tried to sell the logbooks directly to the market. I was so obsessed with making my money back from the Easylog venture that I burned a year or two trying to recover my costs rather than calling it quits sooner. I kept telling myself that I could make it happen—that I just needed more time to sell my product, and then I'd make my money back.

Trying to sell the product direct to market was very time-consuming, but I couldn't quit because that meant that I'd have to accept the loss, and I just couldn't do that. I believed that if I sold directly to market, I could do better, but that cost me another $60,000. It was not a viable product to be sold independently; it was better suited to a sales environment with a bigger distribution channel. The device was a low-cost, high-volume item that made small margins. So, unless my advertising efforts resulted in high-volume orders, there wouldn't be enough money to cover the advertising.

I was starting to panic, doubting whether I could turn things around. My friends tried to support and motivate me, telling me stories of how many successful entrepreneurs went bankrupt before they made their millions, but it only made me feel worse.

It took me a very long time to let it go, and when I did, I eventually sold the whole stock to someone who sold customized logbooks to the trucking industry for $15,000, just to get rid of it. That was the slow and painful death of my Easylog vehicle logbook product. My goal went from selling my product to paying back my financial losses.

My business loss took a toll on me—mentally, physically, and spiritually. I lost the fire in my belly, and my spirit was broken. My thinking became twisted. It was as if I was operating from a whole new set of values. I had no idea how to get myself out of the financial mess I was in and felt I had nobody to turn to. I had a desperate energy about me, stuck under a growing debt of $300,000. My future looked bleak.

The whole experience was a massive learning curve for me. Commercializing products and getting them onto the shelf requires a lot of capital. There are so many restrictions on distribution; you need warehouse management and stock management. You have to develop relationships with distribution vendors, wholesalers and retailers. It was so much more involving than I had realized.

In hindsight, it was a very bold move. I was new to the game, completely raw, but I just went for it. I wanted to experience the idea of products just selling themselves off the shelves, but I didn't know nearly enough about that line of business. Another rookie mistake.

A key lesson was that spending a lot of time developing your product does not mean you have a business. If you can't repetitively sell your product or service, you don't have a business. I also learned about opportunity cost. That is, while I was wasting time trying to recover my losses, I was missing out on the opportunity of what I could create next.

My first business failing was certainly the toughest for me. I believed in my products and intended to succeed. No one intends to fail. But when you win at something you don't look back and analyze it; when you fail you contemplate what went wrong, and ask yourself, "What could I have done differently?"

Looking back at this experience now, I made a very important shift of focus from creating physical products to creating service products.

In 2000, I flew back and forth to Sydney to sort out my issues with Easylog. In November of that year, my sister, Petra, who was working for the Anthony Robbins company, was attending the

"Unleash the Power Within" seminar in Sydney, and as I was there, I decided to join her.

One aspect of Tony's teaching is using the science of neurolinguistic programming to help people understand themselves and create change in their lives. NLP describes how the mind and language affect our body and behavior. It's quite an in-depth coaching tool and is highly recognized. It helped me delve deeper into understanding my belief systems, improved my decision-making and created movement in my life. I opened myself up to what Tony was teaching, and it is ingrained in me now. After attending his seminars, I felt like I could make a billion dollars.

Also, in Sydney, I underwent the transformational program called Landmark, which guided me through breakthroughs and shifts in my life. Where Landmark grounded me, and helped me to become more "real," Tony's programs helped me to dream big. Attending seminars, applying myself in business, and my self-directed learning efforts all played a big role in shaping who I was at that time.

After all the trips I took to Sydney in 2000, about eight in all, I fell in love with the place. Sydney hosted the Olympic Games that year, and the city was buzzing. I was mesmerized by its bright, colorful beauty. I called all my friends, enticing them to join me in Sydney while I was there. "Hey, man, the weather is better, the beaches are spectacular, I have no hay fever here. You gotta see this place!"

One day a friend said, "You're always glorifying Sydney—if you love it so much, why don't you move there?"

I hadn't contemplated moving there because I had my Industry Outplacement business in Melbourne, as well as my family and friends. But when my friend posed that question, I thought, what's stopping me from living in Sydney? I extended my business trips, staying for a month or two in serviced apartments around Sydney to get a feel for the city, to see if I really loved it—and I absolutely did. I sat in a restaurant and wrote a list of pros and cons of making the move. The pros won. My decision was made. I was never going back to Melbourne. I moved into a two-bedroom apartment with a sunroom in Double Bay, ten minutes from the city.

I felt as though Sydney was the right environment, the right breeding ground for my creative endeavors and my entrepreneurial mindset. I was seduced by its beauty and drawn to its spirit of big business and enterprise.

I chose to live in Sydney and that changed my life. Here I was, twenty-nine years old with my birthday fast approaching. I'd been told that I wouldn't make it to thirty, but I was at my peak of physical health. I only worked about four hours a day, doing most of my business between 10 a.m. and noon, and between 3 p.m. and 5 p.m., as people were not available in the middle of the day. I was looking after my health in a big way at this time, and I felt great. I'd go for a run or go to the beach at lunchtime. I swam, did a bit of bodysurfing, and worked on my tan. It was an exhilarating time.

I celebrated my thirtieth birthday in March 2003 on Shark Island in Sydney Harbour with 120 friends. It was fantastic, a real celebration.

I had proved the doctors wrong.

However, I knew I had still not achieved my goals. I had even gone backward. I felt frustrated because I'd wanted to make my first million by the time I was thirty. Most of the inner conflict in my life was about trying to fit into a life I didn't have, which was about making money. My thirtieth year was a hard one for me in many ways, emotionally and financially, but I was determined to just keep going.

Through the Easylog venture, I discovered my talent for marketing. After that I read everything I could about sales and marketing. There was no way I could go back to a nine-to-five job to simply pay off my debt. That seemed like a complete waste of time.

For most of 2003, I immersed myself in marketing—or should I say, wheeling and dealing. By that I mean jumping into any transaction I could get my hands on. No matter what the job was, I found out a way to get in between deals and be paid a commission for it. For six weeks I worked for Tony Robbins, selling his seminars. I got to know Michael, the main promoter of Tony's events in Australia, and did a few deals with him. I printed T-shirts or sold tickets on the side when he wanted to boost sales. I sought out this type of work with other promoters who represented different speakers and got involved in other industries providing marketing mail-out services, helping people buy expensive equipment and organizing labor hire.

I often used Bartercard money to exchange goods and services with people. I called it my "funny money" because it wasn't real money. The Bartercard money was easy to generate and sometimes I would convert it into real money as profit. According to their website, Bartercard "allows business owners around the globe to conduct business without the use of cash money. Businesses use Bartercard's own digital currency as a way to conduct business that allows them to conserve cash as well as move excess stock.

At one point I had a large amount of Bartercard money that I was looking to convert to Australian dollars, to realize its value in the cash economy. I took advantage of a Bartercard promotion for a hotel on the Gold Coast offering rooms for 100 percent Bartercard money. Considering I was scheduled to volunteer at an upcoming "Date with Destiny" Tony Robbins event on the Gold Coast, I was able to see a possible deal happen by packaging up a budget accommodation alternative for those attending the upcoming event. I pitched the idea to Tony's promoter in Australia. "You're going to get more ticket sales because the Palm Meadows Golf Course venue is expensive and there are no accommodation options nearby."

He agreed on the condition that I arrange buses to take the guests to and from the venue every day. We agreed, and I eventually had two busloads of guests. With my Bartercard money, I paid a total of $80,000 for the rooms (which were priced at $80 per night) and paired up women with women and men with men in each hotel room with two single beds at $45 a night. During my five-day volunteering stint, I had made more than $100,000.

That deal came together well, but my wheeling and dealing efforts didn't provide a steady income. I'd make $20,000 in some months and in other months nothing. I lowered my living expenses and managed to survive without getting a nine-to-five job. I still ate fancy meals, went out and lived my life normally, but when the deals were running low or cashflow was drying up, I limited my expenditure. I lived on peanut butter sandwiches and two-minute noodles a few times. In times with little income, I found myself thinking about my debt and becoming stressed about it. I also became much more determined to pursue an entrepreneurial path in life; any other options seemed irrelevant.

In Sydney I met a lot of people in different industries. Rob was a full-time doctor and was making money on the side, working from home doing affiliate marketing online. He was earning large commission cheques from generating enquires online. As an affiliate marketer, he would represent a range of companies and get paid differently depending on their commission offering. In early 2004, I asked him to teach me how he did it. "Rob, if we can record how you make money on the Internet, I can create a curriculum from what you did, and we could sell that as a step-by-step course on CDs."

"I'm not interested," he replied. He didn't believe I could sell it.

"If I could sell the course to ten people for $2,000 each within a couple of weeks, would you consider it?" He agreed to give me a go. I spread the word about the course, writing letters and explaining what it could do for people, how they could make money with affiliate commissions by advertising online. To my surprise, I sold it to twenty-five people at $2,000 each and made $50,000 in two weeks—before we even developed the course! Rob reluctantly agreed we had to do it.

We set about creating the course and over the next six months I broke down his information into modules and created CDs and workbooks, and there we had it: the kit for the Online Marketing College. I ended up selling that course to hundreds of people over the next few years. We did seminars and sold it off the back of other people's seminars also. Rob was the speaker, and I promoted it. I invested a lot of time and energy into that business. I knew that it would inspire me to pursue the "lifestyle business concept" of working while traveling, doing business online—a long-held dream.

CHAPTER 5

A New Way to Think, a New Way to Live

B usiness was doing great. The online marketing business was going well, we had staff, and I felt as though I was picking up the pieces of my life and becoming the successful entrepreneur I'd always wanted to be.

In mid-2005 I had a headache that wouldn't go away for two weeks and was taking Panadol for pain relief. One day, when I went to the toilet, I felt something was not right when painful electrical shocks ran up through my spine. I had to contort my body to pass a motion and avoid the incredible pain. It was a strange and frightening experience.

Rob advised me to get checked out immediately. "Mate, something serious is going on; you need a scan."

I didn't connect the pain with the VHL diagnosis because I'd been ignoring it for the past ten years. I had the scan and went straight back to work at my office.

The doctor's office kept calling me, but I was so busy I ignored them. "You must come in before five o'clock," the receptionist told me. She called me at three o'clock and again at four.

"Do you want me to come in now?"

"Yes, Chris. Immediately," the receptionist said.

Oh no, I thought. It could not be good news.

My doctor said, "Chris, we found the reason for your excessive headaches, and we've taken measures to have you operated on urgently."

"Why?" I asked her.

"You have a massive five-centimeter blood tumor in the back of your brain," she said. "You've really let this go. The tumor is so big that you could die from this at any moment. If you exert yourself in the toilet, or if you fall and land on the back of your head, it could burst, and you would die. It may burst any day."

I shook my head in shock.

"Today's Tuesday, and we've booked you in for the following Thursday with one of the best brain surgeons I know."

"I'm having a brain operation?" I still couldn't register the severity of it.

The doctor nodded. "Yup."

Holy cow!

I walked out of the doctor's clinic and screamed to the sky, "Enough is enough. God, you might think it's my time, but I'm not going to let this get to me. I'm not going to let this be a disempowering moment in my life. Try to kill me, but I choose life."

The following day I met with the surgeon who was going to cut into my brain; I freaked out. "Doc, this is really personal, you're going to cut into my head, operate in my personal space. This is an invasion of my being."

"Look, you'll be OK because the tumor is not in the middle of your brain," he replied confidently. "It's only in one area on the edge of your brain, beneath your skull. We just have to make a small incision, cut out a little bit of the brain, and the tumor should come out quite comfortably."

After the operation, I woke up feeling mostly normal. In the recovery ward, doctors and nurses asked me to touch my nose and move my hands, testing for side effects from the surgery. I thought they were silly. "What do you mean, touch my nose, and move my hands? Are you guys crazy?" I was able to do all those things. Yeah, I thought, I dodged a bullet. I wasn't going to die.

A few days later, the doctor came to my hospital room and updated me on how the operation went. "Chris, it all went as planned; I made a slight cut on the edge of your brain, drained the tumor, then pulled the sac of skin with all the blood vessels out in one go. It all went smoothly."

It was such a relief knowing that I was fine. Yes, I was a bit sore and wobbly, but otherwise, I was great. For the first two days, I felt floaty and euphoric, with a sense of enlightenment, appreciating that I had a second chance to live. I realized at that moment that if I didn't start living the life I wanted now, then I might never get a chance to.

As a result of the brain swelling after the operation, I developed a kind of extrasensory perception. I was super sensitive to everything and everyone around me, conscious of what other people were thinking or feeling even before they entered my room. It was a bizarre experience, but it was amazing because I had some very interesting conversations with people in this new state of consciousness.

One day I looked out of the window and saw life going on regardless of what was happening to me. Birds were flying in the sky and people were going about their everyday business. I could have died, and the world would have carried on. It triggered the realization that the world wasn't all about me—my existence was insignificant in the grand scheme of things. After the brain swelling had subsided, my special ESP gift went away, but I became more grounded and appreciative of others and the value of life.

After the third or fourth day, I was starting to feel a bit better and went for a walk around the hospital, St Vincent's Private, and the nearby parks. I soaked up the sun's warmth on my skin and embraced my new attitude of gratitude.

I hated the hospital food and called my friends to join me for lunches or dinners in the nearby cafés and restaurants and shops. One evening, I had dinner with a female friend of mine and by the time we finished it was 10:30 p.m. I had to walk back to the hospital, and I was very wobbly. I felt as though I was balancing my head on a pin.

When I arrived back at the hospital, it was closed. There I was, knocking on the door wondering how I was going to get back in. My house keys were in my hospital room, so I couldn't go home either. I pressed the doorbell and told the staff that I was a patient. They didn't believe me until I showed them my wristband. They let me inside, scolding me for sneaking out. I was using the hospital more like a hotel!

The brain operation was my wake-up call to start living my life to the fullest. Every day I looked up to the sky in appreciation, infused with zeal and enthusiasm. Before the operation, I would often restrain my joy, not appreciate the moment; after the brain operation, I let loose. There was no holding me back. If I wanted to sing or dance in the street, I would. I was super, super happy. It wasn't fifty-fifty happiness; it was 99.99 percent pure joy.

No one in the hospital was singing or dancing like me. If you compared me to other patients, they were heavy, and I was light. Lighter without my tumor and lighter in spirit. My attitude was astronomically different to anyone else's in that hospital. My surgeon said he had operated on a lot of people in his time, and only come across a few people who reacted to life-threatening situations the way I did.

Before the operation, I had no idea what I wanted, really. I had trouble making decisions. I would wake up not knowing what wheeling and dealing I'd be doing for the day. I had no set agenda, no set work, no set schedule, nowhere I had to be. I didn't believe in the future. What was the point of believing in the future? I was going to be dead by thirty, so I was an angry young man. I ignored my condition as much as possible and was an example of how not to handle life, in every way.

While in my private hospital room, I had a lot of revelations. I went from being an angry young man to being super happy, from being disempowered to being fully empowered, from not believing in a future to planning for one. There was now a massive sense of urgency to everything. This realization still has an impact on my life even today.

After the operation, I had no shortage of things I wanted to do. I stopped being afraid of making decisions—I made them fast and didn't worry about whether they were "right" or "wrong" because

I knew I could make a new decision. I let go of the fear of failure. I thought, So what? Another costly experience. The difference after the brain operation was that I became all-in or all-out in everything I did in my life.

Facing my mortality put me at peace with my life. I became more receptive to life; I became clearer about what my higher purpose was and accomplished anything I set my mind to. I took care of my outstanding debts and turned my life around.

I didn't have time to be angry, sad, or depressed about my condition anymore. Life is precious. Who has time to be down and out when your tomorrows are not guaranteed? I didn't give any time to disempowering feelings anymore. I had confronted my very survival and felt a deep sense of my insignificance and yet was ready to live life to the fullest.

After my brain operation, the doctors thought I should have a whole-body scan, considering it had been over ten years since I'd had any scans. They were worried that I hadn't managed my condition very well. So, the hospital staff wheeled me in to have an MRI of my entire body.

What they found was not good. Both my kidneys were riddled with tumors and 95 percent of my right kidney was consumed by cancer, with some tumors as large as five centimeters. I met with the doctors, who wanted to take both my kidneys out. I'd been lucky with the brain operation and got lucky again that the tumors on my kidneys hadn't spread throughout my body. Both could have killed me.

"Hold on a minute," I said. "Let's just pause. I need to recover from my brain operation. Give me a couple of months, and then we'll deal with the kidneys." I reasoned that the tumors had been in my body for the past ten years, so a few more months weren't going to kill me. I was very blasé about it. It was like, yeah, we know that I grow tumors. It's to be expected.

When I'd been diagnosed with Von Hippel-Lindau syndrome at the age of nineteen, the doctors had also tested my parents for the condition. Dad's test at that time showed up negative. That was the biggest cause of my doubt regarding my own condition. I didn't really believe that I had it because it was supposed to be a hereditary condition. How could I have this condition if my parents didn't have it?

In 2005, while I was confronting these kidney challenges, my family members had themselves tested once more to see if they could donate a kidney to me. To our surprise, not only did my father have cancer in both kidneys like me, but it was also confirmed that he had one of the two types of VHL mutations. People with type 1 VHL rarely have the mutation in some of their cells, therefore it's less severe. There are 3 version of the type 2 VHL, each with their own risk levels that develop cysts and tumors mostly in the eyes, ears, lower part of the brain, spine, pancreas, adrenal glands and kidney and as such is much more severe. The age when these symptoms start can vary depending on the VHL mutation you might have. Mine started at 16 years old with eye angiomas; for my Dad, his symptoms started at age 57 years old.

It was a shock, but we saved Dad's life because his cancer was at high risk of spreading throughout his body, and we got it out just in time. He was only 57 when both his kidneys were removed. He went straight onto the list for a kidney replacement because Australian government health regulations made it impossible to receive a donor kidney after the age of 65.

Dad's illness derailed his career as a production manager at ATCO. His fear about his condition prevented him from building a new career, making it difficult for him to progress financially. It was an unsettling time for him, and he became very reserved. All his life, he had been well-off, but at the end he died a poor man. Seeing how my dad's health decisions affected his quality of life, I determined then that no matter what happened to me, I would do all I could to maintain some quality of life. Even if I was seriously unwell in the future, I'd always look forward to my tomorrows, always find a reason to keep working and to live for my family, for my causes, for my businesses and for the things that mattered in my life.

I know this is easier said than done—I have experienced suffering that can best be described as "scary." I've been tested more than most and I admit I know how easy it is to lose hope and feel helpless in those situations. With many health adversities ahead of me, I asked myself, Am I going to constantly react as a victim of my condition or will I respond as an empowered, committed-to-life individual? Will my future health setbacks wear me down? Will I get to a point of feeling powerless? Could a time come when living with such pain and suffering is pointless?

I know what it is like to give up on life, so the answer is, maybe. This is also why my resolve must be firm to keep living well despite the limited time I may have left, no matter how limited my capacities may be in the future. If you're willing to hope that things will get better in the future, then you might as well even go so far as to believe that the best is yet to come. I have made my decision that no matter what, I choose life.

When I got home from hospital after my brain operation, I noticed the preparations for the annual City2Surf fun run happening just outside the window of my Bondi Beach apartment. It's a fourteen-kilometer fun run from Sydney CBD to Bondi Beach. You would often find over fifty thousand people running or walking the race. Some take the run seriously, others dress up in costumes and make a day of it. I thought, wouldn't it be nice to be a part of that? I had participated in the City2Surf a few years earlier in 2003. I was fit and healthy then and trained hard for it. My target was to complete the race in sixty minutes, but I finished it in sixty-five minutes.

When I went for my check-up, I told the doctor, "I'm running the City2Surf next week."

"What? You must be joking."

"No. Why do you say that?"

The doctor shook his head. "Because you've just had a brain operation in a part of the brain that controls your mobility." He didn't want to say no, don't do it, but he strongly advised me against it.

"Could it be fatal?" I asked.

"Well, no, but it's not advisable. You might seriously injure yourself."

I grinned at him. "OK, so I'm running then."

On the day of the race, I was still experiencing some side effects from the operation and couldn't move my head fully from side to side. I hadn't trained, but I didn't care. I joined the throng at the start of the race, and while I was waiting, I thought, I'm here; I might as well give it a good shot.

I let go of all the excuses for not feeling well. The starting shot fired, and I ran. I did the best I could with every step and every breath. I ran with a spring in my step, delighted that I could move so fast. I couldn't wipe the smile off my face. I embraced the moment, completely focused. I had all the reasons in the world not to do well, not to even finish. But I just kept going.

Twelve kilometers into the run, I ran past some friends sitting at a coffee shop in North Bondi. They jumped out of their chairs, cheering me on and clapping. It was an exhilarating moment that spurred me on even more. I was with the pack of the first one thousand competitors. On a downhill slope, I felt as if I was flying.

As I sprinted to the finish line, I looked at the big clock and thought, Holy cow, I'm under sixty minutes. I ran the race in fifty-eight minutes and twenty-two seconds, breaking my personal record. It was one of those fantastic moments in life when you ask yourself what the hell just happened. Even though my head felt pretty messed up, I celebrated.

Running the City2Surf and breaking my personal record was a transformational moment. I realized how much I'd been underestimating myself in other areas of life, often limiting myself before I'd even begun anything.

I recognized that there is a spiritual force and energy within us that exceeds the limitations we place on ourselves. There is more to us than we think, and there are forces much larger than us at play.

These realizations gave me a new confidence in confronting the challenges of my life and helped me to develop more of a spiritual context for things. When you are faced with near-death experiences, you gain peace with the idea that one day you are going to die, so turn up the music and play. Enjoy the dance of life while you're in it.

I wanted to just get on with things. I didn't want to delay anything in my life anymore.

As I get older and more mature, I'm benefiting from reflecting on my past, and I can make more calculated decisions without overthinking and overanalyzing. I'm far more confident in taking on greater responsibility. I've thought through my past experiences enough to know I'm not going to repeat mistakes over and over in my life.

I have surprised myself with how far I can go. There's a joy in applying yourself wholeheartedly and fully in life, especially when you discover a higher, more empowered version of yourself. I was very mindful that my own personal philosophy and worldview could either be a framework that suppressed my potential or one that strengthened me to take on life on my own terms. I wish everyone could experience this feeling at some point in their lives.

Live up to your full potential

When I woke up to my mortality, I stopped taking time for granted, I had an overwhelming sense of gratitude. Grateful for each day, I knew I was lucky to be alive. From that moment, I didn't have time to entertain all my worries, doubts, and insecurities any longer—I simply shifted my focus. I devoted most of my time to understanding my desires. This gave me clarity around what I wanted to do with my life and why the path I was taking was important and meaningful for me. By doing so, I found the courage to start living a deliberate life, doing what I love, doing what matters, because I had nothing to lose, nothing to fear. After all, I'm not getting out of here alive.

The table below shows how my choice to be self-empowered transformed my life.

Disempowering beliefs (negative qualities)	Self-empowering beliefs (positive qualities)
Often doubtful	Often confident
Disheartened	Inspired
I would rather run away from life's challenges	I am actively taking on life's challenges
Passive, make safe effort in everything I do	I am all-in, active effort in everything I do
Low energy	High energy
Often overwhelmed	Increased control of my life
Low self-esteem	Belief in myself
Limited viewpoint, hard-headed	Open-minded, vulnerable, willing to learn
Frustrated, limited	Motivated, unlimited
Stuck in a rut, over-worrying	Excited about the future

Disempowering beliefs (negative qualities)	Self-empowering beliefs (positive qualities)
Starting but never finishing anything	Creative, productive
Focused on problems	Focused on solutions
Always blaming other forces	Responsible for my own life
Always telling others I can't do it	Often tell myself I can do it

You can't live up to your full potential if you are often doubtful and have insecurities about what to do with your life. It makes it harder to discover what drives us and to recognize our gifts, talents, and passions. Not knowing what to do with our life affects our ability to put our best selves forward. We are less likely to take a chance at something if we are uncertain. It affects our ability to step outside of our comfort zone. Overall, it is our self-confidence—or lack of it—that constricts our ability to live up to our full potential.

CHAPTER 6

Time for Me

My right kidney, 95 percent cancerous, was removed a few months after the brain surgery. After two traumatic operations, I needed time to heal and settle into my new ways of thinking.

As part of my healing, I made the decision to stop drinking, even though alcohol was ingrained in my life. Just as I'd done when I gave up cigarettes, marijuana, and other drugs, I simply stopped (and I haven't touched alcohol since). But I also thought it would be good to remove myself from the Australian drinking culture.

At that time it was all about an opportunity to catch up with friends over a drink every Thursday–Sunday and then recover Monday–Wednesday and start all over again. We were always going to various nightclubs or bars and hanging out with my nocturnal party friends. Someday, even if I didn't feel like drinking, I just did because I wanted to catch up with my mates.

It all made sense for me to take a year off and travel overseas. But I had a few things to sort out first.

While I was preoccupied with the brain and kidney operations, the online marketing business had suffered. I'd always known that if it weren't for me, there wouldn't be a business. Rob was the speaker, we had web designers and technical staff, but I was the one who drove the revenue. No one was doing sales except for me. When I stopped promoting it and working on it, the business came to a halt. For Rob it was just a side project, but for me it was my business. If I was going to take the year off, the only option I had was to simply end the business. That was nothing compared to the surgery I'd gone through.

Another matter I needed to take care of was subletting my Bondi Beach studio apartment to earn additional money. I was lucky that the apartment faced the beach, making it highly desirable for subletting. But it was old and run-down and leaked when it rained. It was a community-living type of place without its own kitchen. I didn't mind a communal kitchen; that's why the place was cheap. I was paying only $190 per week. I targeted travelers and backpackers because they wouldn't care about a communal kitchen either.

I'd bring prospective tenants in and sit them facing the beach. I was selling them the view—and trying to mask the slight odor from the fish and chip shop downstairs.

"Where is the kitchen?" they'd ask.

"Check out this view," I'd reply. "Look, you can see the surfers."

"But where's the kitchen?"

I didn't answer until they asked three times and then I told them about the communal kitchen but again played up the great location and view.

The property manager had often warned me that subletting wasn't allowed, but I did it several times over the next year or two, avoiding trouble because every time I advertised the apartment, it was taken immediately. I experimented with the price until I found a comfortable amount the market was prepared to pay, which was around 200 percent more, at $450 per week, perhaps up to $600 in peak season. As soon as my apartment was rented, I took off overseas.

My first destination overseas took place over December 2005 at Koh Samui, Thailand, to heal and have fun with fifteen of my friends. It has since become a place that I often enjoy going back to in order to fast, eat organic vegetables, lose weight, get fit, on top of it being my favorite remote working location.

Returning to Sydney after my Koh Samui trip, I wondered what I was doing here with only $2,000 left to my name. The brain operation, kidney operation, and the trip had eaten most of my savings away. I asked friends for donations or to use their Qantas Frequent Flyer points so I could fly around the world and was amazed at how many people were happy to help fund my travel and healing time. Friends also donated cash—$500 here, $2,000 there and one friend even gave me $5,000. I was grateful for their contributions, and I believe that sometimes in life it's OK to ask for help.

Rob, my partner in the online marketing course, had set up a new business operation in Cebu, in the central part of the Philippines. I had never been to the Philippines. I knew one Filipino person in Australia. I didn't know anything about the Philippines and as matter of fact I didn't even know where it was.

He invited me to stay over in the apartment he rented with his American friend James, a fellow entrepreneur. James became a dear friend of mine, and still holidays with my family and me today.

In 2006, the Philippines became my first overseas destination that year, starting off my year of traveling. James's apartment was in Ortigas, a major business hub. Being in the Philippines for the first time, I wanted to get out of the city to see the amazing tropical islands the Philippines had to offer.

I was surprised to find people speaking English in Southeast Asia and where my money could go so much further than I was used to in Australia. I saw the poverty, the economic environment, but I found the Filipino people to be happy and cheerful and not embittered by their circumstances.

After a few weeks with James, I was off to enjoy a health spa for a month. I was looking for a health spa somewhere on one of the islands and after an extensive search, I found one in El Nido, Palawan. It's a remarkably beautiful tropical environment with pristine water and beaches. I was excited but the spa was in the center of town on the edge of a beach. It wasn't what I expected or hoped for.

Unfortunately, when I arrived, it was so noisy I canceled my booking after the first night. The owner of the resort, an older English woman, suggested I go with her to her second resort on a private island, a forty-five-minute boat ride away. She told me it was much quieter.

"Chris, it's a women-only resort," she said, "and I'm a nudist, so they have the freedom to go nude if they wish."

My eyes widened in a mixture of shock and delight. "Oh, I don't know if I want to go there."

"It's OK, I've spoken to the other women," she smiled. "They don't mind having you there."

I liked this quirky, old English woman and decided to take up her offer. She was intelligent, free-spirited, and comfortable in her own skin. I loved that she chose to live the way she wanted, on her terms. Her island was spectacular, beautiful, and pristine. It had a beach on each side of the island and lots of lush vegetation everywhere. A real tropical utopia. The resort had five beachfront bungalows.

I spent time with her, sharing marketing tips and helping her out with her website—and occasionally, she was naked. I'd never seen a woman of that age naked before; it was a bit strange.

The ladies staying there always invited me to participate in activities with them.

"Come and do yoga with us, Chris."

"No, I don't think so."

"You can stand at the back," they joked.

"No way."

I went to the nudist island purely to eat healthily and focus on my healing. I spent a month meditating, running, having colonic treatments, kayaking, swimming, and resting. I lost a massive amount of weight—20 kilograms. It was a beautiful time, and I felt great.

While my brain and kidney operation had forced me to look at my health and well-being differently, and I enjoyed taking the time to heal and relax, but a part of me felt I was wasting time. I asked myself, "What am I saving myself from? Why am I giving all my time to healing?" It was that concept of giving *all* of my time, *all* of my life, that I began to question. Imagine giving every bit of your time toward trying to be super healthy; it defeats the purpose of living. What kind of living is that? We're all going to age and die one day, even the healthiest super athlete. If I had limited time, did I really want to focus on health treatments to gain an extra year or two?

I finally came to terms with the enormity of what I'd overcome: my brain operation and surviving kidney cancer. I remembered the words of an old Japanese Dr. Shigeaki Hinohara, who said, "Don't die looking perfect, just live." No one has saved themselves from death yet, so I thought I might as well just get on with life.

After my nudist island stay, I decided I wanted to date more women. I went online and met *a lot* of women. Just like marketing and sales, it was all about the numbers and the conversions back then. The more women I met, the more chances I had of having sex, and in the beginning of my year of traveling, that's what it was all about. In those years, the word *commitment* wasn't in my vocabulary.

And then in April 2006 I met Rica when I returned to James's apartment in Ortigas. Rica was one of the girls I was dating online, and I wasn't expecting anything different from my encounter with her. I told her what I told all the girls: that I wasn't interested in a serious relationship. I was upfront with all the women I met and never led them on.

On April 17 I sent Rica a playful message: "Put on a dress and I'll take you to the Shangri-La Hotel or put on jeans and I'll take you to Starbucks." All the Filipino girls I dated wore jeans and I was getting fed up with it. Some of them were so pretty, and I couldn't understand why they were downplaying their beauty. Girls back home in Australia would dress up to go on a date.

Rica decided to wear a dress. I vividly remember the first time I saw her outside the Ortigas Shangri-La. She wore a red-and-white checked dress with a baby blue top.

The first thing I noticed was how young she looked and how small she was. She had to be under five feet. She'd never been in a fancy hotel before, and I could tell she was nervous. She looked like a baby-faced girl but was super cute and sexy. Being a typical guy, all I could think about was how I could "convert" her and have some fun, but I was really worried about her age.

"You only look sixteen," I teased.

"No." She shook her head. I made her prove her age to me by asking to see one of her IDs and was relieved to see that she was twenty-one. She was quiet, and I felt her observing me, especially when I ordered us iced tea to drink. Later she told me she wondered who this Australian guy was who drank iced tea and not beer or spirits.

I gave Rica my usual spiel. "Don't fall in love with me. I'm not marriage material. I don't intend having children because I have this hereditary condition. I just want to have a bit of fun." My health adversities made me question my longevity in life and so I put up a wall to safeguard me from possible emotional pain. I didn't see anything wrong with sexual pleasure but as soon as there was an emotional connection that went a little deeper than the norm, I was quick to move on.

Rica surprised me. "Well, I want to have fun too." She was more open than the other women I had met, more honest and accepting of my terms and conditions, and she didn't place any demands on me initially.

And she was intelligent, a real bright cookie. I learned that she'd gone to one of the most prestigious schools in the Philippines and won a scholarship to study psychology. When she finished her education, she worked in a variety of customer support roles, and was currently working in a call center.

However, I remember thinking that she was far too short for me.

I enjoyed my time with Rica in the Philippines for a couple of months, but it was time for me to continue my online dating and traveling quest around Asia. My itinerary was based on who I was talking to online at the time. I thought it was a great way to travel. I often had dates lined up before I arrived in a city. I'd check in to my hotel, get ready and meet my date. It was a great way to see the sights of a new city, so I only went to places where there were online dating websites I could use. Back then, they weren't available everywhere as they are today.

First, I flew from the Philippines to meet a girl in Hong Kong. A few days later I caught a train all the way to Beijing to meet up with the women I'd lined up there. As the train traveled north, I noticed that the weather was changing drastically. I hadn't done any of the usual travel research like checking the temperature, hotels, or touristy sites. All I'd checked online were the dating sites. It was a long train ride (most people fly), and I couldn't get enough of the food. None of the signs were in English, so I was constantly asking strangers about which stop was which. It was my first long train trip and the whole thing was a delicious experience.

When the train arrived in Beijing late at night, it was negative one-degree Celsius. I didn't have any winter gear. I put on three T-shirts and used a long-sleeved shirt as a jacket. It was freezing! My exposed skin was hurting from the cold.

It was dark, and everything was closed. It was like a ghost town. I saw a building a few blocks away with the lights on, but thought I'd die of frostbite by the time I got there. I was stranded.

Out of nowhere, a stranger came up to me and asked me something like, "English, English, hotel, hotel?" She grabbed my arm and took me to a nearby van. It was full of other Western backpackers, and I got the last seat, in the front between the lady and the driver. If they hadn't picked me up, I'd have been in serious trouble.

We were dropped off at a local motel and given a cheap room for the night. At breakfast, none of the menus were in English so I just gestured for my waitress to give me anything and received a bowl of amazing noodles. I decided to look for accommodation closer to Beijing's central attractions. But first I went to the nearest store to buy appropriate gear for the weather: a jacket, a hat, a pair of gloves, longer socks, long johns and an undershirt.

I found a hotel near a shopping plaza, a five-minute taxi ride from the famous Forbidden City and Tiananmen Square. I checked in, then went straight back out to explore.

I met a Chinese girl who wanted to practice her English and asked if she could accompany me in whatever I was doing. I thought it'd be nice to have some company over lunch and invited her to join me.

The restaurant's menus were all in Chinese, so I asked her to order whatever she wanted as long as she ordered me one vegetarian dish. The next thing I knew, five large meat dishes arrived. I thought there must have been a misunderstanding. We hardly touched the dishes and when I asked for the bill, the girl asked for the food to be put in takeaway containers.

"I'm sorry for any misunderstanding, but can we split the bill?" I said.

"No money. I take food home to family."

I'd been scammed.

The following day I visited a colorful street market and went on an excursion to the Great Wall of China. Then I left Beijing for Shanghai.

In Shanghai I met local girls via online dating sites who spoke better English. I'd learned my lesson from Beijing and kept my guard up. Fortunately, I got much better treatment from the women in Shanghai.

I was there for about ten days and had a few dates lined up. It was nice to be taken to museums, interesting neighborhoods, and restaurants. It was exciting to travel in this way.

A few months after my Asian online dating travels, I decided to pause my online dating adventures to go to Kerala in the very southwest of India to try traditional Ayurvedic healing treatments. Ayurveda is an ancient form of holistic medicine, with historical roots in the Indian subcontinent, based on the idea that disease is a result of imbalances in a person's body and consciousness. I did my Ayurvedic treatments at someone's private home; I was even eating dinner with a family with two daughters who all followed a special diet and provided daily massage therapy.

After completing my Ayurvedic treatment I made my way to Thiruvananthapuram, at the very south of India to undertake a spiritual retreat and to meditate at an ashram. It was also where I could get cheap food and accommodation in return for doing some work, such as chopping vegetables or gardening for an hour or two. I spent three weeks in one ashram called Bodhi Zendo, practicing Zen meditation for up to five hours a day and practicing "silence," doing work around the ashram and studying in its library. It was a place nestled among mountains in the middle of nowhere. A peaceful, spiritual, beautiful place. I was surprised by how many "professional" clergy were there and only found a few backpackers like myself. I went there because I was a curious young man, but little did I know that India would touch the core of my existence.

In my meditation I was practicing observing my mind rather than engaging it. It was as if I was observing myself as the observer.

By observing thoughts and not entertaining them, I noticed how many doubts and concerns about my future and welfare I'd been carrying with me. I became more grounded in the present, without the anxiety about my mortality and life in general. A decade and a half after being diagnosed with my hereditary condition, I finally gained peace around it and this was a liberating experience, rekindling my hunger for living large.

Since that moment I have recognized just how much more important it is to sustain and manage a peaceful mind and state. I guard my peace. I've stopped my emotions and imagination from getting carried away with worst-case scenarios and circumstances. I've done that for far too long.

By sustaining a peaceful mind, I'm much more present, I am aware, I am focusing on what I can do, how I can respond better to life-threatening situations or business adversities. This shift has transformed my life and has kept me alive longer. A peaceful mind often helps me appreciate the present moment and occasionally has me overwhelmed with gratitude. When my life is full of gratitude, I am significantly more positive, humbled and open to seeing new possibilities.

Live like it's your last year alive

Initially, I was struggling with the popular saying "Live today as if it was your last." This felt too short term; if I only viewed time as one continuous "last day," it gave me anxiety. I couldn't be strategic with my plans, my desires and the use of my time.

So, I changed it to "Live like it's your last year." With this perspective, I can block out time for plans throughout the year. It helps me recognize my priorities in the present moment and brings forward all my decision-making abilities. Thinking in terms of the now and the end of a calendar year has allowed me to improve my creativity and better manage my perception of my mortality. And linking a visual image to a goal allows me to get very clear with my true desires and direction throughout the year.

How I accomplish my yearly goals

Making a conscious choice to design your life instead of allowing it to happen is a process that goes deep—perhaps much deeper than you might think. Our minds respond strongly to images and when we link an image with a goal it can help us to gain visual clarity.

Others refer to this process as creating a vision board. It's like your mental inventory, a reminder of your desires in the long term and in the short term. The idea behind the vision board is to match your actions with the images you placed on it, giving your life a direction.

Create your vision board for the year ahead when you're in a state of reflection and gratitude. Keep your mind at ease during the whole process of creation. Avoid distractions. Wake up early, so you can let your subconscious and your instincts come alive over a period of days as you create your intentions for the year ahead.

The steps below require you to feel your way through it. Don't overthink it. The goal is to find images that align with your intentions and your intuition. Focus on how the images make you feel. There are various methods for creating a vision board. There aren't any rules. You can create one on your own terms, and change it as often as you need, so long as it feels right.

Here's how I go about it:

1. Start by looking for images that get you thinking "what if" thoughts. If the images inspire you, make you smile and make you feel good, take a screenshot, keep them. Do not place images on your vision board that you believe aren't possible for you to achieve.

2. Place one or a few images in relevant categories, such as home, body, mind, spirit, experiences, events, career, finances, leisure, education, family, friends, business, public service. Delete any images that no longer feel right.

3. Now, rate each image on a scale of 1 (low desire) to 10 (high desire). Delete any images that are of low desire. If a particular image on your vision board makes you feel like crap, delete it.

4. The goal is to limit your images to only those that inspire you; five to fifteen images will do. Too

many images can make it difficult for your subconscious to focus.

Your new vision board isn't real until you start scheduling your time to take tiny but consistent steps toward your desires all year round. If you choose to create a vision board, plan around important events such as birthdays, public holidays, events or seasons throughout the year will free you to confidently schedule well in advance.

As you work through your vision board, one goal after another, you'll start getting better at managing the time, energy, and commitment you put into each goal. You may find yourself working on some goals simultaneously.

As often as you can, spend the last hour before you sleep each night visualizing and believing in your goals. Do not skip this process: it has a jet-fuel effect on accelerating what you can manifest.

Setbacks are inevitable and are part of any progress. Know that you're not always going to deliver on what you said, so don't be hard on yourself. That just makes unnecessary stress to carry the pain, burden and regrets from the past. It's OK. Learning to let go of something fast is one of life's most important skills. Forgive yourself. It's all good so long as you're alive. Tomorrow is a new day. A new day equals a new go. Try again. Just keep going.

From Thiruvananthapuram, in the very southwest, I made my way to New Delhi via train and got a flight to the far north, Kashmir, to check out the Himalayas from the border of Pakistan and India. It was a fascinating two-day train trip that was much different than the ride to Beijing. The train cars are divided into many classes—Unreserved General Class, Second Seating AC, Sleeper Class, Three Tier Air Conditioned Class, First Class Air Conditioned Class, Executive Air Class and so on. In Unreserved General Class, you find people on top of people and crowds everywhere. It's too intense. I ended up in one of the nicer classes. It was a colorful experience and an incredible way to see the scenes and the various landscapes of India. India is so diverse; the country has twenty-two official languages and over one thousand different cultures.

I remember beggars, especially kids, asking for alms on the train. There was a kid who had a disability, deformed in some way. He freaked me out because he was able to maneuver like a spider underneath my seat and then between my legs to ask for money. After I shooed him away, I saw him do the same to other passengers, reaching them by making his way under the seats.

There was this bearded, very masculine-looking man dressed in a white dress, kind of like a transvestite, who demanded attention. Before he entered the train car I was in, a kid played a drum to announce his entrance. As the very masculine-looking man walked around the train car, he stared intensely at each passenger, including me. Another kid (or perhaps the same kid beating the drum) started asking for money from the passengers, and everyone obliged, even myself, because we were scared of what the very masculine-looking man was going to do if we didn't.

A few hours later, the train stopped in the middle of the night in New Delhi. The massive train platform was covered in a sea of bodies of sleeping people on the floor. They were barely clothed—no shoes, just poverty to the nth degree. I got off the train, and I had to walk over them. I even accidentally stepped on a young boy, a teenager. I remember when I stepped on him, he woke up and said it was OK. He was just so nice and happy, lit up. If this were Australia, he would have been a junkie or something. I got to see this kind of happiness in people from the Philippines but it was just so shocking to see in India.

From New Delhi, I got a flight to Kashmir. When I landed, I was unaware that fighting had broken out. I hadn't been watching the news. I went through about twenty passport checks before I even left the airport.

Army vehicles and tanks lined the streets. Shops were boarded up and no hotel was operating. There were soldiers everywhere. I could hear gunfire in the distance. The airport bus dropped me off in the center of town and that was the only time I saw a few civilians. One guy approached me and asked about my situation. For a small fee, he offered to put me up at his house, which happened to be on a houseboat. The following morning, I needed breakfast and wanted some good coffee. The houseboat family told me there was a place I could get breakfast and coffee further down the river, so I tried to make my way there.

Along the way, as I was walking, I came across a barricade where a soldier stopped me and said, "You can't go over there, there's shooting, and a sniper might kill you. You have to stay in the city and in a building to be safe."

"Yeah, but I heard that there's a breakfast place where I can get coffee further down on the river."

"But that's a five-minute walk, and you could be shot," the soldier argued.

"Yeah, but I really want a good coffee, man."

He said something on his walkie-talkie in Indian to the effect of, "Australian. Coffee. Cease-fire."

Suddenly, the firing in the surrounding hilltops stopped.

"You've got five minutes," he said. "Hurry." He opened a gate to let me pass but said, "If you get shot, we can't provide medical aid. Don't come screaming to us if you get a bullet."

He made it clear that I was on my own and that freaked me out. He opened the boom gate, and I stood there terrified as I realized how horrifying the situation actually was. It was very real. Clearly, I hesitated and thought twice, but after arguing for so long, I felt obliged to follow through on my decision.

As I started walking to the breakfast place, I couldn't believe that this soldier had somehow managed a mini cease-fire just for me. But as I was walking, the silence terrified me even more and I started running to the little shop by the river. There were a few people inside, barricading themselves in, but otherwise the whole area was deserted except for soldiers. After all that, I got my breakfast and coffee, but it was really bad. It certainly was not worth risking my life over.

The following day, I was eager to get out of Kashmir and go to Leh. I was lucky to get the last seat on the bus that was taking off moments before I arrived. The road from Kashmir up to Leh had to be one of the most treacherous in the world. It was a dirt road cut into the mountains. We were surrounded by a surreal mountainous landscape devoid of trees.

I thought I was going to die on that journey; it was more frightening than the possibility of dodging bullets in the Kashmir war zone. The scenery was spectacular, but the bus just fit on the road, winding its way up the steep mountainside. The bus journey lasted two nights and three days, with a stop each night in a small town. I was cramped in an uncomfortable seat with my knees hitting the seat in front, all the while I was adjusting to the altitude. Everyone except for the bus driver got altitude sickness. I passed out at one stage, waking up thirty minutes later with a very bad headache.

We were so high we could look down on other mountains, but then we continued up and up. It was incredible. When we pulled over to rest, I lay down on the grass and was astonished to see a sign marking the road as the second highest in the world. It was a relief to learn that we were descending from that point.

After that crazy bus journey, Leh was so lovely. Leh is 11,483 feet above sea level. I stayed in Leh for five days to acclimatize and another five days to prepare for a hiking trip in the local mountains. I spent $400 on equipment: special kettles, water purification stuff, all the necessary gear. I enjoyed that place in the remote mountains and meeting fellow adventurers.

I kept up my meditation ritual of one hour at sunrise and one hour at sunset. I wanted to maintain the amazing presence and awareness I had developed at the ashram. I learned to observe my reactions and respond to people in a more conscious and compassionate manner. I remember how light my spirit and energy were. I felt euphoric, climbing mountains, being physically active and meditating daily; just me giving time to me—100 percent.

I explored the villages decorated with prayer flags and climbed for hours alone, feeling on top of the world. It was a magical experience, but it was so isolated that if I were to get even the smallest injury, I could have been in serious trouble. I practiced climbing without winter gear to about five thousand meters above sea level because anything over five thousand meters often got too cold. I wanted to prepare for Base Camp at Mount Everest, which was six thousand meters above sea level.

I was planning to do a ten-day solo trek from Leh, but my cooking mechanism broke. It was a stack of pots that clamped together, but it broke when I tested it. I really needed the pots to be able to cook food for myself out in the middle of nowhere. Also, with the clamp broken I couldn't stack the pots together to fit on the outside of my bag. If I put them inside my bag, everything would get dirty. This minor problem ended up being a major blessing in disguise. It literally saved my life.

The next day it rained heavily in an area that apparently had not seen that much rain in over two hundred years, and the plains flooded. If I'd been out there, I would have been stranded if I was lucky—or I might have died. People were stranded overnight on top of their cars, roads and bridges were wiped out, and a seventeenth-century temple was destroyed in the flood. I'd had my sights set on doing the trek, but I was so lucky that my cooking mechanism broke and delayed my departure.

I'll never forget my time in Leh. What impressed me the most was the gratitude people had for little things. You were grateful for someone serving you a meal or fixing your room. I was a paying customer and of course money was important, but the intangible qualities of kindness, care, attention, recognition and awareness were more respected and more valued. Money and our busy lives often distance us from the humanity of life and the rewards that spring from that.

I met a lot of hippie tourists who recommended I go to another ashram in central India to meditate with one of the popular gurus at the time, Sai Baba. I went but chose to stay in a hotel beside the ashram because I found the whole "guru" thing a bit weird. I felt safer having my own space.

The phenomenon of Sai Baba's effect on people was fascinating. The ashram was like a spiritual theme park, and there was a whole town of people who worshipped this guy like he was a living Jesus.

Imagine if Jesus, Muhammed, or Buddha were alive right now, walking around on earth. Imagine the hysteria. The town was swamped with memorabilia: key chains, fridge magnets and all these quirky things sold as a souvenir of Sai Baba's presence. There was that materialistic, making money side to it, but it was the spiritual side that blew me away.

Imagine a large tract of land with a massive community where people would live just to be around Sai Baba. Everyone wore white, but he wore orange and stood out even more because he had a big Afro.

He did the same thing every morning: He'd be driven on a buggy into a big hall, and just sit on the podium, smile, look at people, and then go away. I did note that he tried to look at everyone, but whether he looked at me was hard to tell. People waited for hours for this. He'd say nothing, and then he'd walk away. All these people sat there, praying and meditating, sure that by being in his presence they could feel the power of his healing in some way.

There was a mysterious worship room at the Sai Baba ashram that took me four or five days to finally enter. After spending three or four hours praying, meditating, and worshipping, you go into a special room where a crowd of thirty people gather to chant. It's remarkable. By that point, you're ready to be in that room. But Sai Baba isn't even there—the room is decorated with posters of him.

I was in that chanting room for maybe half an hour, but it was unforgettable. I experienced a deep feeling of love and spiritual warmth and could sense all my chakras (centers of power in our body) opening. I remember tingling and other bizarre physical sensations—probably to do with the meditative state I was in.

In that little room it became clear to me that your thinking is such a small fraction of your consciousness. Something occurred beyond my understanding. And then I was abruptly brought back to reality. In typical Indian fashion, someone slapped me on the head so hard that I said, "Ouch, that hurt." Then somebody else roughly grabbed the back of my shirt to lift me up. They weren't subtle. They literally used their feet to kick us out of the room. The incongruity of it was comical.

This experience made me question my faith. If Jesus were alive today, would I worship him like that? Many of us worship some god or religion but worshipping somebody intensely, in the flesh, is bizarre to me. Almost cultlike. Modern-day worship is convenient. You go to a church or a mosque now and then, but would you kiss someone's feet? Would you wait all day to be in their presence? Would you devote your whole life to someone? The funny thing is that I do worship my God in my mind or heart-space, but it made me question how I would act if I was to see him in the flesh.

After my experience with Sai Baba, I made my way to Rishikesh via train. The train ride was a day and fifteen hours. After finding a place to stay, I went for a walk to explore the local area and found a fourth-generation Hindu psychic, clairvoyant, and birth chart astrologer.

He agreed to have a session with me. I put on my poker face, determined not to give him any information. Then he said, "You have a sister and a brother."

"No," I told him. "I don't have a brother."

"You do."

"I think I'd know if I had a brother," I joked.

"Call your mother before we start the session, then. Where are you from?"

"Australia."

"Call your mother," he insisted. "And ask her for the time of your birth."

I called Mum and asked her if she had a third child that I was not aware of.

"Chris, I thought you knew," she replied. "I had a miscarriage."

I was shocked. I asked Mum about the time of my birth and then told her I had to go.

When I returned to the psychic, I asked, "How the hell do you know all this?"

This man now had me hook, line, and sinker. He told me how my sister was going on a cruise, how she was considering a new haircut, how my father had kidney problems and how someone much younger than me had fallen in love with me. He said I'd continue to travel, make more money than I could dream of, and how people would come flocking to me at one point in my life. What he didn't pick up on were my health challenges. It was as though he was looking at my future through a crystal ball and just calling it. When I look back, I see that he was accurate in just about everything. It was an uncanny experience.

In Rishikesh, I was catching up with an Israeli girl who was staying at the same five-dollar-a-night hotel as I was. We met at a coffee shop right across the street from the hotel. She was on rest and recreation leave from military service in Israel.

We had a table on the edge of the coffee shop against some balustrades, and below us were people sitting on the dirt. I didn't feel comfortable with where we were sitting because the people sitting below us looked like junkies and I was worried they would steal my friend's bag. I asked to be moved, but all the good tables were taken. The people sitting below us were so close I could have touched them with my foot, and I'm sure they heard every whisper of our conversation.

After my friend left, a skinny old man sitting on the dirt got up. He had a long white beard, was barefoot and had nothing on but a sarong. He looked like he'd gone through tough times. He said, "Excuse me," in a refined voice that sounded like an English lord, which didn't match his appearance.

Surprised, I looked at him on the other side of the balustrade. "Yes?" I replied.

"You foreigners are all the same," he said.

"Tell me, guru, what's up?" I sat back in my chair and sipped my drink.

"You're all looking for love," he said as he waved his hands. "I can see that you're looking for love."

"No, no, I'm looking at her ass," I answered flippantly.

"You're not looking at her ass. I can see you're looking for love. But you have to *learn* to love first." He looked at me longer than what felt normal. It was intense. I stared back at him, dazed. I hadn't been really paying attention to him at first. I was just at a coffee shop. But when he knew he'd made an impact on me, he left. And that was it.

Later that night, I reflected on his words. I let them simmer and sink in. There I was, in a random coffee shop in the middle of India, in the middle of nowhere, and that one conversation slapped me in the face: "Wake up to love."

I'd previously thought it took a miracle to fall in love and that was something you looked for outside of yourself, but this new realization was that love was abundant, and the secret to finding it was a question of how receptive you are to it and *learning* to love.

I'd been mucking around like any other typical guy, but after that encounter, everything changed. Dating wasn't about fooling around anymore. It became an experiment with this concept of learning to love the person in front of me.

I was learning to love, but I also fell in love. I fell in love with a lot of the girls I dated after that, and with people in general. They were all from various backgrounds, some pretty to look at, some not. Big, small, tall—they were all beautiful. I asked myself what I could learn to love about each of them. Every new date became an exercise in learning to love. I realized that it was not difficult to love. It was a lot easier than I'd ever thought possible thanks to this simple change of perspective about love.

Interestingly, I remember the girls I dated after India much more than the ones before, because I was opening my heart and experiencing what it was to love other people. Where I once was horrified by the idea of commitment, the knowledge that I could learn to love someone finally allowed me to be willing to commit.

So, the question I asked myself was, how do I decide who I could love and commit to a lifetime with? Who was most appropriate to continue this journey with me? I imagined myself with Ms. Shanghai, Ms. Saigon, and Ms. Philippines. I thought about the qualities I liked about each woman and the things that irked me. I began to think of every woman I met in terms of how well we could work as life partners, in the hope that it *could* be a lifelong partnership.

Even though you can learn to love anyone, it's harder to love some and easier to love others. Love is a choice. I wondered, who are the ones who are easier to love? Who was the person who could complement my personality and add value to who I was, and vice versa? I went through a whole series of processes and assessments on the idea of love, but the answer soon became loud and clear. I didn't have the control over it that I thought I had.

After five months in India, I flew back to the Philippines to be with Rica for a month. She booked me a cheesy little apartment in a seedy red-light district. We hardly left that apartment, and really bonded, simply enjoying each other's company. I felt I could be me with Rica and felt happier being with her than I had been with any other woman.

I brought Rica with me to Koh Samui and a few other places as we were getting to know each other on a deeper level. It was one of the happiest times of my life.

Initially, I didn't think Rica was my "ideal" woman, but she had qualities that I discovered were important to me. I was starting to see her as a possible life partner. She was a woman who was easy to love; loving Rica seemed natural and effortless. And I was easily able to resolve any personal and emotional issues with her. She was a free spirit, anything goes. Communication is so important. I never experienced any roadblocks with Rica like I did with my family or others I've known over the years, and that's amazing. There was something about her that was unwavering and I felt peaceful and comfortable with her. I loved her family values and her personality. She embraces who she is in every way and is unapologetic. She provided me with the room for my own self-expressions and independence.

CHAPTER 7

New Beginnings

Home from my whirlwind romance with Rica in the Philippines and Koh Samui, I could not get her out of my mind. My feelings for Rica had grown, but while I was serious about her, I wasn't ready to commit totally because I wanted to get to know her more.

While she was visiting me in Australia, I was the gracious host, and we did everything together. One day, out of the blue, Rica stormed out of my Bondi apartment. I was surprised and perplexed. What happened? I tried to call her but no answer. Then I saw that she'd been using my computer and had found my journals about my travels and experiences with other women.

She just took off without me. I went looking for her and in and around Bondi Beach, almost a one-mile stretch of beach. I didn't know where to look, I was wandering around. I finally found her curled up in a ball on the grass, fifty meters from the beach.

We went for a walk and sat on the cliffs overlooking the ocean. She had been crying and was clearly distraught. We had a heart-to-heart conversation, and I was honest with Rica about everything. I explained what life had been like for me growing up with my career and life-threatening challenges, and how having that year off was about healing, but also about living. I was wary of commitment partly because of the question of my mortality.

There were tears, and I had to be careful how I explained myself because the truth of it was that she could have left me. I had to be prepared for the consequences.

I knew that we had the potential to create something magical together and were building a foundation for that. I didn't want to damage what we had. I could already see how she was impacting my life in such a positive way.

I had never broken anyone's heart before. I never wanted to hurt anyone. I thought, What the hell am I doing? I didn't want to lose her. Despite Rica's distress, we agreed to move on and work on our relationship. It would take time to repair and rebuild the trust.

The fact that Rica was still committed was mind-blowing. It seemed I couldn't shake this girl. She loved me enough to forgive me. I was touched by her strength, determination, and commitment to me.

This episode hastened my own decision about committing to her, but I didn't tell anyone yet. I wanted to make sure it was the right decision, so there'd be no regrets.

My initial intentions for traveling around the world had been much the same as for any other guy. I was going to have a global adventure, shag and have fun. Before 2006, I thought it would take a miracle to fall in love and make the decision to love someone. In reality, love is abundant. It's everywhere. The question is, how receptive was I to love? And how open was I to learning to love? That random encounter in India changed my view of the concept of love.

I learned very quickly that love was not me trying to find it in somebody else, but it was already *in* me, and it was my ability to *learn* to love someone that was more important than love itself. The whole notion of love clicked for me. When we learn what it means to love, we are finally learning how to connect on a spiritual, emotional, and mental level. The physical happens to be the least important of those connections. This was the first time I had experienced such an emotional connection and delved into these other realms in a relationship with anyone—it was scary and exciting.

I took my decision-making process about marriage slowly and methodically because I had a limited lifespan. I wasn't sure how long I'd live. Equally, marriage was a lifelong decision, so what was the rush? For a period of a year, I wanted to pause and observe my decision to marry Rica.

It wasn't that I was still trying to make a choice. The choice was already made. But I wanted to sit with it, to see what it felt like and if it was still the right choice at the end of a year. It took time to go through layers and layers of understanding. Was I making this choice for the right reasons? Was it my choice, my family's expectations, or society's expectations? The process entailed deep, dedicated focus and thinking. And all the while, my commitment to Rica was deepening.

Rica was so intelligent. I had spent so much time and money on personal development and was amazed that when we discussed various topics, she not only understood but was able to effortlessly apply new concepts to her life. She was like a sponge, absorbing everything, and growing mentally, emotionally, and spiritually. She was so open and adaptive, willing to go along with her new experiences. There was no culture shock. It was that trait that deepened our relationship more quickly. It was incredible. She was incredible.

Sometimes you don't know how you will feel about your decision until you've made it real by telling others about it. One day I randomly told the owner of the fish and chip shop below my apartment. He just knew Rica and me as customers, but he was ecstatic for us. I observed my internal responses to telling a few people about my decision. Combining all those unique responses for over a year helped me solidify my resolve to commit to Rica fully. It's not an approach I've seen anybody else do. After a year of this observation, there was no inner conflict or resistance.

When my right kidney was removed in 2005, one of the doctors told me I had to have the left one removed also. Another doctor suggested that the kidney should be cut in half, and the third one said he could remove the tumors while retaining as much as 85 percent of the kidney using a different procedure. I thought I should get a variety of opinions from different hospitals and from doctors who did not collaborate in any way. A friend recommended that I visit a surgeon at Westmead Hospital, about an hour away from St Vincent's and Prince of Wales Hospital, the hospitals where my doctors were located.

This new surgeon recommended taking a more conservative approach, addressing my kidney problem in two stages. The first stage involved radio frequency therapy for the small tumors. Stage two would be an operation to remove the big tumors a year later.

I decided to go ahead with stage one and went to Westmead for the procedure.

While I was recovering from the kidney surgery, my friend Mark, who was being promoted by a wealth creation company at that time, was unhappy with his marketing results. Mark was presenting a property investment scheme, and in six months the wealth creation company had only been able to get thirty-six attendees to pay $1,000 for his property seminar, and that was with a staff of fifty and a large database.

I shared my experience about working with Dr. Rob and said to Mark, "You know what? I reckon I could do better for you." I then proposed that I redesign his property wealth creation seminar.

So, I redesigned his seminar, repackaged it, added double the value, and as a result sold it at double the price to triple the number of people who paid to attend, and achieved all this in half the time. On top of that, I didn't have a team of fifty people, or any database to start with. I did it all on my own.

I spent two months developing the website, the sales material, the marketing plan, and coordinated everything. Then I spent just one month marketing and selling the seminar to achieve this spectacular result, which helped Mark launch a new speaking career and go on to make amazing new profits on the back of my marketing efforts.

After I'd successfully promoted Mark, our partnership fell apart because he felt I was too greedy in our arrangement. But the reality was I'd done such a great job that I became obsolete. Not only did our partnership fall apart but so did our friendship. Mark was the first friend I lost as a result of making a lot of money. It's a sad irony that out of the businesses I failed in I never lost friendships, whereas through this success I lost this friendship.

After the partnership collapsed, I gained confidence in my marketing abilities, and this gave me the fuel to take my entrepreneurial capacities to a new level. I stopped deliberating about what it was that I should do next. I got results. I didn't wait anymore. All I had to do was just create more. In a free market, there is no one stopping me from making whatever amount of money I want. No matter how many personal disadvantages and concerns I might be worrying about, none of them matters to the market. The market doesn't care about my intelligence, weaknesses, or my education.

Earning simply is a function of creating value and solving problems for others. This insight was the shift or the turning point that created wealth for me.

The wealth creation company was so impressed with what I'd done for Mark's seminar that they offered me a marketing consultant position. The owner of the wealth creation company, Jamie, is also an incredible marketer. What I loved about working with him was the fact that whatever we thought or conceptualized, we just ran with it and made things happen. And he trusted me; I was his go-to marketing adviser.

Rica was able to extend her Australian visa on her second trip to Sydney and I got her a job working with me at Jamie's company.

Jamie and I collaborated on strategies for his concepts. I had to understand the product he wanted to create and see it as a finished product in my mind. I can't remember all the details of the specific products, but they were mostly around creating money from the stock market, Internet marketing, business, and real estate. I had to consider the target audience and use the right language to encourage people to buy the products. Much of what I did to influence people in marketing had to do with taking a position with what we were representing and backing it with facts. Then I'd present these concepts in a rough format to Jamie, and he'd then assess which of these things he could deliver on.

I enjoyed using my imagination and felt there was no limit to what we could create.

On stage at his seminars, Jamie would say, "Look, I'm going to present some of our product concepts," and he would attempt to sell these and garner feedback. After this I would create follow-up marketing material to further his concept. I helped create some of the curriculums for his educational products. These were all about helping people acquire new skills to improve their lives via their own self-education efforts, something that really resonated with me. We had a lot of fun earning hundreds of thousands and sometimes millions of dollars' worth of sales from products we believed in.

Jamie hired me to take care of his marketing affairs, but his team didn't want to be managed by me because they were inspired by Jamie and in awe of his celebrity status. This was frustrating at times. I tried to find a solution to this issue because Jamie was spending so much money on marketing. I decided to hire my own dedicated marketing contractors to operate for him. Toward the end of 2007, I contracted thirty people in the Philippines to work for me online—project managers, business developers, web developers, SEO experts, customer support and administrators. I put them under my company and Jamie agreed that I could contract them out to him. I paid their wages and invoiced Jamie, and he paid me back.

I also assembled a local customer support team for Jamie's business. Rica worked as part of the local team.

I realized I had provided a great business solution and birthed a whole new venture. This was the genesis of my new company Remote Staff. It took some months to put the business together but it was at this point the seed was planted in my brain.

Everything was going well for me. I had the seeds of a new business, and I loved being with Rica. I loved Rica!

To me, love was and still is a mystery. I don't fully understand it. It's deeper than logic; it comes straight from the heart. It has made me do things I'm not used to doing and become more generous. I've done a lot of things out of character because of "love." As a result, love clashes with my ego, but love always wins. I often jokingly complain about love for that reason.

I never thought I'd have a family because of my hereditary condition. But Rica changed all that. So, in 2008, when I was thirty-five, I knew it was time to propose.

The wealth creation company Rica and I were working for had a business event in Noosa on Queensland's Sunshine Coast. I decided to surprise Rica and propose to her in this beautiful place. I told the crew at the company about my intentions and asked if Rica could come along under the guise of it being a business trip. Rica thought it was odd that she was going but I insisted that it was for "business" and that she was needed.

I went to a lot of trouble planning for the proposal, which I thoroughly enjoyed. I had Rica's engagement ring custom made in Thailand months before and hid it from her. I booked a hotel room at a resort on the beach next to one of my favorite restaurants. I booked a table and organized with the restaurant management how I wanted the scene to pan out. I gave them our favorite song and cues for when to stop everything so I could propose.

The next night, we went to the restaurant and were seated at a lovely table. The restaurant was packed, and the atmosphere was very pleasant, but I was nervous, trying not give away what I was about to do. I was sweating.

There was a live pianist. After we were done with our main, I gave him the cue without Rica noticing. The pianist then started playing our song. A spotlight shone on us. Rica still didn't notice. I got out of my seat and down on one knee. I was prepared to devote my life to this woman and was happy to kneel for her.

Rica wasn't sure what was happening and looked around. The whole restaurant was staring at us. She didn't notice I was on my knees at first because I was the same height as when I was sitting on my chair.

"What are you doing?" she asked. "Why are you on your knees?"

"Rica, will you marry me?"

"Are you serious?"

When I look back, I laugh because I was expecting a "Yes" straight away, but she kept repeating, "Are you crazy? Are you for real?"

"Yes?" I asked.

"Yes!" she said.

I looked at the piano player and nodded my head.

The pianist made an announcement on his microphone. "This gentleman has just proposed! Let's congratulate the new couple." People got up out of their chairs, clapping and yelling out, "Woo-hoo!"

We were embarrassed by the unwanted attention, so I asked for the bill without even finishing the desserts we had ordered. We both wanted to get out of there quickly. We ran across to the beach and laughed hysterically about what had just happened. I thought that proposing in public would be a good idea. I'd seen proposals on television and thought it would be fun. But I don't know why we do that, because it's such an intimate moment, such a special moment between two people. It's not meant to be a spectacle in front of a whole restaurant.

I felt a whirlwind of emotions. We talked about our decision to commit and build a life together. We had a wonderful celebration, and I was overwhelmed with joy. I was amazed that I had found my life partner, that I loved her so much. I believed we could build a future and foundation—for a tower built upon our love.

CHAPTER 8

Living the Dream

Now that I had found the love of my life, I wanted to enjoy the remote working dream with my fiancé. I wanted to live and work to the beat of my own drum, immersing myself in different cultures and not being the rushed traveler that I so often saw. I wanted to meet locals and embrace the local way of life no matter where I was, and to savor the experience while working and expanding my business.

This remote working dream was what spurred me to start the Remote Staff business. Rica and I were traveling at every opportunity, like migrating birds. Over the next few years, remote working and traveling became our lifestyle. I would choose a country and locate us there for a couple of months just to experience what it was like to work and live in that culture.

When you're a tourist, you have the whole day to explore and do touristy things but you're only in a place for a limited time. You're often in a rush, squeezing as much as you can into a day. But when you're remote working, you're there for longer. For me, it's about doing the things I would do back home, but in a new place.

Rica is less keen on it, as she struggles to get into the mood to work in some environments, especially tropical islands.

At first, I didn't know how long I should stay in a new country. If we stayed for two or three weeks in a place, it was just short of satisfying and was more expensive. It was easier to negotiate monthly accommodation rather than a daily or weekly rate. I found that if we moved too frequently, we suffered a feeling of displacement. It was hard to constantly find quality Internet, accommodation, and travel needs. Moving around frequently became too much to manage.

I learned that six weeks was the sweet spot. It took that amount of time to truly get the feel of a place, to befriend some local people and get to know the streets, the shops, the prices and popular things to do. A six-week stretch could also incorporate a couple of weekend getaways. So, if we were in London, we'd zip off to Bath, or if we were in Paris, we'd go to Nice for the weekend.

Sometimes we stayed in places for three or four months, but I felt that if we were going to stay in a place for such a long period of time, we might as well be at home. The goal wasn't to settle in a new place, just to get a feel for it.

What's important to me is seeing life through different eyes. Of course, I see the world through the perspective of my own history, background, values, and experiences, but I'm very interested to understand what makes other people tick—their worldviews, perspectives, and culture. Drinking a coffee in Africa is a different experience from drinking a coffee in Paris.

When you stay in a place long enough you see what people will tolerate. In the Philippines, I'm shocked by the long lines of young people waiting patiently for a bus or "jeepney," but they don't complain. Try finding a line like that in New York!

When in Paris we would rent a one-bedroom apartment that was opposite a restaurant. Every morning a man would play "La Vie en Rose"—seeing life through rose-colored glasses just outside our apartment. Framed photos lined every wall, it was very artistic and very French. The apartment was private and practically soundproof. Every time I opened the windows in the morning, the scent of fresh bread and the sounds of the café and the man playing his romantic song filled the apartment. Paris was amazing environment for me because I love the architecture, bread, and the hustle and bustle. There I was with my wife, working remotely on my business feeling like I was earning my worth for the day, and yet I could then shut my laptop and look at this world. We enjoyed watching the people and observing how they dressed, and went to restaurants and tried different foods. Who doesn't love the French? French people don't typically like to try to speak English, but with me they really tried to communicate because I'm so open and warm and friendly. I was inquisitive and curious and I loved everything about these environments. You would go to a place that says "Cheese Shop," and that's all they sell. We don't have many shops that just sell cheese in Australia. They would have three hundred different cheeses. I would end up spending hundreds of dollars in euros to buy cheeses; they were more delightful than chocolate, these flavors were amazing.

Being open to all these different experiences is like living multiple lives. Not many of us are lucky enough to experience such diversity or to be shaped by different environments. You are who you are, but if you live in the mountains your lifestyle is going to be different from how it would be if you lived in a big city. I've seen how different environments really do shape people.

But even though I love working remotely and have explored many places and cultures around the world, I still choose to live in Sydney. Australia is home. In late 2007 I returned to Sydney to take care of the second stage of my kidney management plan—to remove four big tumors in my remaining left kidney.

When I met with my surgeon and he explained the process, I asked, "Will I have another ten years of life on a third of my original kidney?"

"It depends on a lot of factors, but two to ten years is the most likely outlook."

"Get me ten years and I'll employ thousands."

The doctor was surprised by my comment but ignored it and continued with the diagnosis. When I was about to leave his office, he asked, "By the way, how many people do you currently employ?"

"None."

Four months later, in February 2008, I went under the knife again. My body was cut open from the front of the ribcage around to the back. The surgeon went in and sliced the tumors off. He was able to have a good look at the kidney to make sure that no new tumors were growing.

It took me three months to move properly again because the incision affected the muscles around my ribs. I found it difficult to breathe. It felt as if I'd been attacked by a shark, or somebody had put a big human-sized clamp on my lungs. I still have an impressive scar around my body.

Before my kidney surgery in February, I left Jamie's wealth creation marketing company, but continued to contract out the 30 staff. After the operation I thought about my noble pledge—something I was honor-bound to fulfill. A few months later, I contracted a group of people in the Philippines, but this time the staff would be working directly for my new business, and this was the start of my Remote Staff business.

The business happened to coincide with the global offshore staffing boom. The development of information and communication technologies meant that jobs that could be done online or over the phone were exposed to international competition. An offshore staffing industry sprang up, and my Remote Staff business was a part of that.

Business owners who hire offshore staff from lower-income parts of the world, such as India, Eastern Europe, or the Philippines, strengthen their business operational capacities without breaking the bank. My business helps our clients access talent from around the Philippines and we work hard to build and maintain trust so that these remote working relationships can flourish. Without trust, improvements in productivity just do not occur for our clients, because without trust they don't have team members who believe in their vision, who work in accordance with their company values or who care enough to look after their customers. It's this essential element of trust that enabled my business to evolve in providing the full service, from sourcing professional talent from the Philippines to providing human resource management and payroll—as well as providing ongoing customer support, compliance administration duties, monitoring technologies, and offering staff retention solutions to sustain the offshore remote working relationships.

I'm very passionate about my Remote Staffing business because as employers we have the opportunity to do global good. I've seen the impact of how we can help our fellow entrepreneurs and business owners grow their businesses and gain more confidence to take on more market share with a team of Filipino remote workers we hire for them. It's our job as employers to help our staff reach their full potential and succeed in the jobs we have them fill. Regardless of if we hire somebody in the Philippines or America it's still up to us at the end of the day to elevate them to become a productive team member who can deliver for our clients at the standards we set.

I'm also passionate about the impact we make in the lives of our remote staff workers. Providing remote job opportunities in the Philippines helps the staff support their families in an alternative work arrangement, alleviating arduous commutes (normally one and a half hours each way), and the hardships of finding and maintaining traditional office-based employment. We have seen over the last fifteen years how our remote workers become valued team members of our Australian, American, Canadian, British, and European clients. Secure remote jobs keep families together and improve quality of life.

I am inspired to help fellow entrepreneurs accomplish their dreams using offshore talent through *remotestaff.com*. Being married to a Filipina, I am also inspired by Filipino family values. Filipinos are committed to their family obligations. If you give Filipino workers a bonus, it goes to the family. This really inspired me to do something to help the remote workers look after their families better.

Thanks to the COVID pandemic, the world has rapidly adopted remote working, with many businesses now choosing to remain permanently remote. This has helped the offshoring industry play a more integrated role in an organization's back-office operation. Traditionally, offshoring was about cost-cutting. Now that offshoring is becoming a main way of doing business around the world, I see the key factors determining the future advantages of offshore staffing to be (1) increased productivity, (2) increased operational efficiencies, and (3) accessing a diverse range of talent for businesses to sustain being competitive. And COVID has also done something else. It has forced many Americans and Australians to reexamine their careers. Many people have gone out of the workforce.

In America it's harder than ever for businesses to find talent. Many people in America and Australia strive to make a difference and bring meaning to their lives and they're revaluating how they do that. They've stepped out of the workforce to either upskill themselves or consider working in a completely different direction. Many employers are struggling to find enough talent. It's perfect timing for the business services I offer, to provide an alternative solution for hiring.

I am often asked, "So why the Philippines?" Apart from falling in love with my wife, I fell in love with the country, its people, and the unshakable Filipino family values. The Philippines has forty million people of working age, with an average age of twenty-five in 2022. The workforce is educated (with 96 percent English literacy), trainable, adaptable and has an excellent work ethic.

The more you understand Filipino culture, the more you can build a strong team—united, cooperative, and loyal—on the back of Filipino family values.

To Build a Performing Filipino Team, Understand Their Culture here are some observations and recommendations—some general, some specific:

1. They will not tell you what they really think, especially if you are the boss, and they will hesitate to go against the majority. Therefore, it is important to hire a local manager or representative, who can be a kind of father or mother figure. They prefer to work in a hierarchical, top-to-bottom management structure. And this is why at Remote Staff we have mature account managers to take care of HR-related matters for you.

2. Filipinos, like any staff member, like following clearly defined instructions. This is important even more so in the Philippines, and if you want your staff to be proactive, you have to explicitly tell them so. It's like they want permission from you to be proactive. Set parameters as to when they can make decisions without your approval. This is not a 100 percent scenario; this doesn't apply to everyone. This kind of thinking applies to about 80 percent of the Filipinos I've worked with.

3. Working remotely with Filipinos requires a lot of relationship building. You will have to make them feel

safe and valued—more like a family member than an employee—for them to open up to you. Once you've gained their trust, they will be motivated to work for you in the same way as they would for their family and in my opinion this is why Filipino workers are loved around the world.

4. Celebrate important holidays and occasions throughout the year—birthdays, Christmas, New Year's Day, Holy Week, and so on. Of course, this is important for many cultures around the world, but it is particularly important for Filipinos. It's important to have a heads-up on all their holidays so that you don't get a last-minute absentee employee and you can still make your deadlines on time.

5. Filipinos are sensitive and tend to avoid conflict by always saying yes. And this is typical of a lot of Southeast Asian cultures.

6. Only 3.5 percent of Filipinos have private health insurance. Therefore, family is always a top priority for Filipinos. When family emergencies happen during work hours, expect your Filipino remote workers to take a leave of absence. This is part of their culture. If there is a family member who has to go to the hospital, there needs to be a family member with them by their side right away. In this developing nation, medical emergencies are not the same. We inform our clients of this at Remote Staff so that they can find compassion for the situations. Just like there are typhoons that they can't control, this is another part of

their culture and their landscape that you have to be aware of.

7. Family pressures and expectations are high. You will most likely be working with a family breadwinner, so know that they are expected to not only cover their immediate family's needs but also to provide for their extended family or other relatives.

8. They prefer to communicate indirectly or to be the last one to speak. Look for nonverbal cues such as raised eyebrows and smiles. This is just something to be mindful of. They are not going to speak up or be the first to share ideas even if they have them. You must explicitly ask them for ideas.

As mentioned, it was love that brought me to the Philippines. However, I'm aware of other developing nations and the price they pay in terms of arduous commutes and sacrifices they make to look after their families. That's why I'm keen to apply my staffing solutions in the future to other developing nations.

Eight months after I started the Remote Staff company, I had Rica join me in October 2008. I couldn't wait for us to travel together, even though this wasn't her dream; she longed to settle and build a life in one place. But a few weeks after she went full-time with Remote Staff, we started traveling.

Rica was great to work with. She focused on operations and fulfillment of the job orders while I drove the sales and marketing front. I was focused on my strengths—strategies, ideas, solutions, and the logic behind what we should be doing in the business. I determined what we were going to accomplish and why.

Rica was a godsend. She became the voice of how everyone really felt, a kind of intermediary between me and my staff, giving me insight into working better with Filipino people and their mindset. She was effective in getting everyone aligned to what the successful delivery of the job looked like. I initiated systems and processes, and Rica and the Remote Staff team developed them. My initial directives now only represent about 20 percent of the work and the rest has evolved because of the team.

It became evident that Rica's strengths lay in systems and business analytics, operations, and technology. While not a developer, she was very good at instructing the development team from a business perspective. She was able to integrate our business needs into our technology processes, so she moved from her role in operations to accounts, and then to the IT team, and eventually as the GM of the company where her skills are best utilized.

Rica is very family-oriented, and she came with a whole set of pure, innocent values about family. My mum, dad and sister, Petra, loved Rica from the first day they met her. Our family was turbulent, but Rica started to smooth out our family issues, bringing us all closer.

After Christmas in 2008, Rica and I went back to the Philippines to tell her family the good news. It was the first time I met her parents, who lived in the province of San Carlos (Pangasinan), four or five hours north of Manila.

Rica's parents, Rico and Linda, her brother, Roy, and two sisters, Rodelyn and Rochelle, are a lovely family. I wanted to do the right thing and ask for their permission. "I'd like to take your daughter's hand in marriage," I said to Rico and Linda. "I have proposed to her, and we'd like to have an engagement party."

They looked at me with blank faces. Having an engagement is not common in their family.

Rica translated for me: "OK, have an engagement party, but what about the wedding?"

I didn't know. I wasn't even thinking about the wedding at that stage. It was a big enough step for me just to propose.

"When's the wedding? When are you going to have children?" they asked. I understand the older generation; they've been there and done that, they have had their families and they're very practical about these things.

"Hang on a minute. Family?" I scratched my head. My decision entails a family? I hadn't really thought that far. "What's the rush?" I didn't really care about the wedding. To me that was just a formality; the most important thing was the decision to dedicate my life to Rica.

I was thinking we'd get married toward the end of the year, but everyone kept asking about our wedding date. Rica and I had had little fights previously, but nothing compared to the fights over the wedding. I relented and we brought the date forward.

So, Rica and I got married on May 23, 2009, in the spectacular setting of Discovery Shores on Boracay Island in the Philippines. Boracay is a beautiful beach with fine white sand. The water is crystal clear. Such incredible beauty. We had our wedding right there on the beach. I was thirty-six years old. With Rica's help, I hired a special wedding planner and we arranged everything to the last detail—Rica just had to show up exactly the way she wanted it. I'm known as a good event organizer, and I took pride in arranging a wedding that no one would ever forget. There was a customized buffet and a stage built with music and performers and fire dancers. It was quite a show, beautiful. The after-dinner celebration was one to remember as we danced the night away and had a lot of fun with friends.

I had my family, my aunt and uncle, and twenty friends come from Australia, as well as my American friend James. The rest were on Rica's side. We flew about forty of her family and friends to Boracay. Coming from a small rural village, none of them had been on a plane before.

All up we had about sixty guests, and we organized a great holiday experience for them. The whole experience was magical—a joyous celebration and one of the happiest days of my life.

Achieve deep satisfaction and fulfillment

Living life without a purpose can feel dissatisfying, empty, and meaningless. You may find yourself unfulfilled, accomplishing one thing after another. It can easily have you feeling depressed and withdrawn.

The doctor I'd seen at age nineteen had led me to believe my life might be over by thirty. This was followed by a period when I was unfulfilled, with no idea what I wanted to do. I felt hopeless. I thought I might die without finding something I could enjoy doing that was important enough to make my life count in some way. I was forced to find my purpose and passion fast. I thought I'd found them when I decided to become an entrepreneur, but it was the making of that pledge when I bargained with my kidney surgeon that shifted my focus from short-term to long-term goals; from self-interest to selfless commitment; from ego to empathy, love and generosity. I didn't realize it at the time, but my adversities—and making pledges—became my superpower.

Living a purposeful life awakened me to a new level of enthusiasm and excitement every day. I felt an inner strength and power, knowing I had a meaning and a direction for my life. I no longer felt like I was wasting time, and my life, away. Anxiety around my mortality doesn't matter to me anymore because I'm doing something meaningful and purposeful. I am grateful and appreciative for being alive every day.

Achieving a deep sense of well-being and fulfillment is a journey of self-discovery that starts within us. We often don't know what is right for our life until we've experienced something that didn't work for us. Things going wrong has often helped me learn what is right for my life.

Having a vision for my life, using my skills to contribute to the greater good, having a loving family and living a purposeful life is a combination that helps me be comfortable with myself—with all my imperfections, weaknesses and insecurities. It's so liberating to fully understand yourself and to be your authentic self.

How do you discover your purpose?

Your purpose is not something to determine quickly. And as you age, you'll need to go through a continual process of reframing and recalibrating your true desires so as to keep moving in the right direction. Once you get an understanding around the five ideas below, they will be important for you—whether you are alive or dead.

1. Let's start with the end in mind: One day you will no longer exist. If you had one year to live, what things would be most important for you to do? Your secret desires are no good to anybody in the grave.

2. You're not getting out of here alive, so why settle for the status quo? Understand what you're made of by dreaming big—it's the fastest way to reach your full potential.

3. Let go of the past to make way for new changes.

4. Build your awareness of the things you enjoy doing. Listen to your heart.

5. Understand your values. They don't change.

Once you have an inner authenticity and can trust in yourself, you can focus on problems outside of you. The world is full of problems; the big question is which one matters enough for you to do something about it. Are you pulled toward something to care more about than most, to be more curious about than most? That could be your purpose.

CHAPTER 9

On Fatherhood and Family

After our wedding, we went to Scotland. Two of my closest friends gave us a honeymoon package: a stay at Dalhousie Castle, a few hours away from Edinburgh in Scotland. Everything from bedsheets to furniture was recreated or restored to how it was hundreds of years ago. The castle was on a large estate with beautiful landscapes and rivers. The dungeon had been converted to a very fancy restaurant serving traditional Scottish food, which Rica loved. It was so different from our lives in Australia or the Philippines. We were like little kids running across the fields. It was only four days, but it was the happiest honeymoon anyone could dream of.

Then it was back to remote work and traveling around Europe, particularly London, Rome, and Paris. In London we'd work in the early morning from our Notting Hill apartment, where I often got complaints from an elderly neighbor because I was so loud on the phone. Then we'd explore the city. We loved going to the colorful Portobello Market and living the London lifestyle.

Our weekdays were busy, but our weekends were magnificent, with trips to places like Bath, Cambridge and Oxford, cities steeped in history and culture.

Rica is a bookworm and wanted to laze around in the parks and read, but I suffered from hay fever, and it would irritate me nonstop. It was funny—I didn't want to sit on the grass, but she loved it. She fell in love with English gardens with their manicured lawns, so very different from the lushness of the tropics in the Philippines or the native flora of Australia.

In 2009, Rica and I traveled for thirty-six weekends out of the fifty-two in the year. That's a lot of weekend traveling—flying here and there, checking in and out of hotels. It was becoming tiring. On average, I was scheduling six to eight months ahead of time because I couldn't organize all these massive trips and events at the last minute.

I'm a big fan of scheduling. My theory is that time moves fast, and if you don't schedule to fit what you want into your life, it will pass you by before you realize it and things might not be viable anymore. So, I always knew where I was going to be and what I was going to do six months ahead of time.

We were in Paris when my accountant called me and said, "Chris, did you know you've made your first million?" Finally, this goal I had worked toward for so long—becoming a millionaire while maintaining a nomadic lifestyle, traveling, and working remotely, and building the business on my terms—had been achieved. That night, Rica and I celebrated like millionaires.

The following month we were in Rome in October 2009. Rica and I decided to have a baby. I called my genetic doctor back in

Australia to share our decision. She told me, "As a VHL carrier, you have a fifty-fifty chance of passing it on to your offspring."

Rica and I discussed going through the in vitro fertilization process so that we could prevent our child from having the VHL condition. Because the IVF process involves fertilizing a woman's eggs with sperm in a test tube, it allows the doctors to test if the embryo has the VHL condition. This would allow us to make a decision about whether or not to implant.

We really had to think carefully about whether we should have children or not. How I had learned to cope with this adversity as an adult would be very different from having a child who had to deal with it. That would be heartbreaking.

We made a decision, and we had a plan. Rica was going to stop taking the pill. We presumed it would take six months or more to get pregnant, which would fit in with our being in Sydney to start the IVF process. However, things don't always go according to plan. By the time we got back to Sydney a few months later, Rica had missed a period. Every day for ten days, she tested herself because she was so excited.

"Oh my God, wifey, I reckon you're pregnant. I reckon we got a boy." We went to visit my family in Melbourne for Christmas, and just before Christmas lunch Rica shared how she hadn't had a period. That was it. Mum and Rica went to find a pharmacy on Christmas Day to buy *another* pregnancy test kit.

And so, on Christmas Day in 2009 we found out that Rica was going to have a baby. It was the best Christmas present any of us could have wished for. It was a joyful surprise; we weren't expecting to have a child naturally. Yet it was a deep, soul-searching and very emotional time for me. We were given an option to do a test to see if the embryo had the VHL condition, but I didn't want to be faced with a decision on whether to abort the embryo should it test positive for the condition. I didn't know I was so strongly pro-life. Who are we to make that call? I have the condition and I am alive. I am worthy of life. And so was our potential child. We might have all the technology to make the decision either way, but I felt strongly about life, so I decided not to have the test done.

Rica, on the other hand, didn't want us to think about the child having the condition at all. Doctors advised us not to test for the genetic condition until our child was two. So, we held off.

I battled with my thoughts. I wanted this condition to end with me. I asked myself, are we worthy of life when we have this condition? I may be bringing a child into this world with such a poor health prospect. Look at me: I've had brain and kidney operations and I see the doctors every few months. I've learned how to live life and move on without the guarantee of a long life. A normal person can expect to live until they are eighty or ninety. They don't really question that. But there's a cloud following me around constantly. I know it's going to beat me eventually, and that's tough to live with. It might not be this year, but every year I wonder if this is the one. I always do my medical check-ups and scans around December, because I want to know that the year ahead is clear enough for me to pursue life to the fullest.

Through this soul-searching, I came to realize that there are worse things than this. Just because I have this condition doesn't mean I can't have a successful, fulfilling life. It doesn't mean that my child can't either. I have to look for positives to balance the negatives. Yes, this is a terrible condition and it's heartbreaking to the core, but will his condition prevent him from living a life that he chooses? No. Will he be able to live a good life, despite his condition? Yes. Might he die an early death? Who knows? But with technology advancing ahead of us, might he be able to live a little bit longer? Perhaps. A positive is that we as a family know how to manage the condition because of everything I have been through.

I had come to accept the whole prospect.

While we were grappling with all of this, my father had good news on his health front. As you may recall, my father had both kidneys removed after I had my right kidney removed in 2005. After four years on dialysis, waiting for a kidney donor, Dad finally got the phone call one morning at six o'clock. My parents were beside themselves. Seeing my father on dialysis was always difficult for me because I knew that one day I might have to face the same experience. He helped me in terms of preparing me for what could lie ahead. I was already clear that I didn't want to be on dialysis for a long time.

When Dad finally got a kidney transplant, we started to celebrate life a lot more. The initial reconnection with my father began in 2005 when I had my first kidney operation, and he was first diagnosed with cancer. A lot changed between us back then because we recognized that we were on a similar journey. We began to look at each other with more compassion and understanding.

When Rica and I returned to Melbourne for Dad's sixtieth birthday, things turned around for us as a family. I really began to appreciate my family for who they were. But it was Rica who really helped us all become closer as the years went on.

Rica had a healthy pregnancy but when it was time to give birth, she had to have an emergency cesarean because it was a breech birth. I was in the operating room by her side the whole time when she had her epidural. They covered her with a big blue sheet from the neck down, so we couldn't see what was happening. We were discussing business when the doctor interrupted, "Excuse me, your baby is here!"

At 10 a.m. on August 22, 2010, I looked into the beautiful brown eyes of my son Jay. He cried when he came out, but as soon as I held him in my arms, he stopped crying. He stared straight into my eyes, observing me. Here was this little person who I was going to know for the rest of my life.

Everything changed for me. Suddenly, the welfare of my son and my wife was more important than anything else in the world. I felt a strong urge to become their protector. I changed from being a person who pursued his own desires and pleasures to becoming more than happy to take on the honor and obligation of looking after my family.

Mum, Dad, and my sister flew in from Melbourne. It was a momentous occasion because Jay was the first grandson. What touched me the most was seeing the joy in my father's eyes. He was the first man in his family to witness the birth of a grandson from a son; all the other men in his family line had passed away at a young age due to the hereditary condition. He was the first one to live long enough to be a grandfather.

But there was a tinge of sadness for my parents—they were denied the opportunity to spend more quality time with their grandson, partly because we lived in Sydney and partly because we traveled so much.

During many of our travels, Rica had suggested that we invite my parents along with us. I wasn't sure about that at first, but in September, a few weeks after Jay's birth, and with Dad recovered from his kidney transplant, I flew them to the Gold Coast to join us for a holiday. It was like a trial run for traveling with my parents and our baby.

I'm so glad we did it. We traveled with my parents many times after that. I feel proud that I had the chance to fly them around the world and to experience some amazing moments together. Dad always had a desire to travel in his retirement and it was an honor to help make that a reality. He and I got to know each other again, more as friends than as father and son, and we healed old wounds. I'll always be grateful to Rica for that.

In June 2011, we hired a motorhome and drove all over Europe, starting off in Munich, Germany. We drove around the southern parts of Germany before making our way to northern Italy. In Milan we met up with my friend Rob and his partner, Marina, and they joined us on our adventures, all together in a six-person motorhome, which felt like a big truck. They were impressed at how we traveled with the baby, Jay asleep on Rica's lap at the back.

Rica and I are real foodies, and we followed our taste buds around Europe. We were intrigued by how much the Italians loved their food. Near Naples, we met a sixth-generation olive-farming family. They had such an interest in and knowledge about olives. When I tried one of their olives, which was almost the size of a big plum, I couldn't believe how juicy and tasty it was.

The next year, we enjoyed our second motorhome adventure, which was inspired by one of the food and travel shows we loved watching. Rica loved sardines and was amazed at how wonderful the sardines in Portugal looked. Since her birthday was coming up, and I wasn't sure what to get her as a gift, I said, "Let's do a motorhome drive around Spain and Portugal. We can go to that shop that was in the TV show. You can have the sardines for your birthday!"

"Are you crazy?" said Rica.

"Let's do it!"

We rented a luxury motorhome and drove more than five thousand kilometers around Spain and Portugal, through the forests, beautiful countryside and small coastal towns, getting a feel for the people and their way of life. I love driving, so the long road trips each day were an absolute pleasure, not a chore.

We love motorhome adventures because we're free to explore and go where we please. It's incredible.

We started off at Barcelona, went all the way north to San Sebastian, and drove through all of northern Spain until we came down to Lisbon, Portugal. Then we traveled to a small town at the southern tip of Spain called Cadiz, where the popular flamenco dance was born, and discovered that everyone went off for a siesta in the middle of the day. Everything shut down; it was like a ghost town. Where was everyone? They were either sleeping or on the beaches. It was fascinating to me, that a town could just shut down. And then at night, they all came alive, partying and celebrating.

When we drove around Spain, we weren't used to the siesta habit. So, we explored the old towns and villages while everyone was having their siesta because it was peaceful, and we felt as if we were the only ones in the world at times. I found it comical at first. I thought, what, I can only eat before 1 p.m., after which everything shuts down? What, I can't have dinner until after 8 p.m., are you for real? What about my baby? It was a different way to live.

People were out and about the whole night, especially during the summer. It was interesting. I enjoyed it but we couldn't keep it up because we usually went to bed at 10 p.m., and woke up at around 6 a.m. The locals didn't get to bed until 3 a.m. and woke up just before lunchtime to have their breakfast.

During our 2011 European trip, we flew my parents over to help us with Jay at one point and then we all went on a weeklong Mediterranean cruise. We booked it at the last minute, setting off from Venice, visiting Croatia, the Greek Islands, including Santorini, and parts of the Italian coast. My dad and I walked the monumental walls of Dubrovnik, a one-to-two-hour walk, stopping at cafés along the way. Mum and Rica went shopping with Jay. While we were walking the walls of Dubrovnik and catching up, Dad told me, "It has been my dream to come here ever since I was a kid. Thank you, son, for making this dream a reality." It was one of the rare moments that Dad talked about his dreams, and what a heartfelt moment it was.

Even though it was difficult to do remote work properly because of the unreliable Internet on the ship, we loved it. It was the first time any of us had been on a cruise ship. We loved the fact that we could use the boat as a base to explore new destinations daily. We'd go out and explore for the day and come back in the afternoon to use all the luxury benefits of the boat, like the excellent meals. And I loved being able to treat Mum and Dad. That was the first of many times when we flew my parents over. They were convenient babysitters—but they had a great time and were a delight to travel with as well.

Rica's mother, Linda, was and is a great babysitter too. She comes to live with us in Sydney for periods of time. Linda loves to travel, explore, and take selfies. She loves to share stories and is very enterprising. A retired teacher, these days she keeps herself occupied buying and selling secondhand goods and making a small margin. If she hadn't dedicated her life to being a teacher, I can see that she would have done well in business.

Rica and I established a pattern that worked for us. For five months of the year, we worked and traveled in Europe, and then for five months of the year we lived in Asia, mostly in Thailand and the Philippines. In Thailand, we'd stay at Koh Samui, for the island vibe, the beautiful food, the freedom and the good quality Internet. I'd also go to a spa there to fast, drink juice, eat healthy vegetarian food and look after myself.

I'd try to make life as comfortable as possible when we moved around. We traveled with an entourage: a nanny, and sometimes my mother-in-law, cousins, or sisters-in-law. To enjoy the same standard of living as we do in Australia I paid a fortune in some areas, much less in others.

The nomadic lifestyle has been my dream—to be able to work and grow a business from anywhere, having a purpose, a mission and creating wealth, all the while traveling the world on a great adventure.

When I started, there weren't many options for digital nomads. Now you can negotiate with your employers to work from any-where as long as you show up at certain times. Most digital nomads live their life focusing on the freedom it brings rather than the financial rewards. I wanted to enjoy the nomadic lifestyle *and* be wealthy. I've accomplished that dream for a decade now.

This lifestyle has also shaped my wife and son. Jay has been traveling ever since he was born. He's been to more countries and done more things in his young life than most people do in their lifetime. When we think of Jay's milestones, we remember, "Oh, we were on the cruise ship when he took his first steps," or "We were in Paris when he first said, 'Dada.'" He had his first birthday party in Koh Samui, and we have fond memories of him running after birds in Barcelona. It's a shame he doesn't remember most of it, but I'm sure it's impacted him and helped shape him in some way.

People were surprised by how much we traveled with Jay. A few of my friends didn't want to travel because they had children, and we were able to show them that it is possible. Jay slowed us down, no question, as we had to carry baby bags and push prams. It was also much more expensive to rent serviced apartments or multiple hotel rooms when family members came along to help, but even though I was paying more in costs it was still worth it. We were having adventures. My philosophy is, why stop living just because you have a child? Bring the child with you and keep traveling and exploring the world.

Jay was a good traveler. He wore his seatbelt, wasn't restless and didn't complain. There were a couple of episodes where he completely lost it as a baby on flights, but I've learned from those experiences. I became strategic—planning flights around his waking hours and avoiding them during times when he'd get sleepy and restless.

When Jay turned two, we flew back to Sydney for a few months to get him tested for Von Hippel-Lindau syndrome. My misgivings about having children came up for me again. Now that we were about to test Jay for my condition, I was dreading it. I didn't want my son to go through what I am going through.

We had to do a lot of crosschecks of DNA between my dad, me, and Jay. Dad gave samples in Melbourne, and we did the test in Sydney. The following week the results came in. Jay's blood test results were negative. What a relief, we were all beside ourselves. It was a blessed and euphoric moment. There would be no early death sentence for my son. He's my son, he's a version and an expression of me, and now he could carry on with his life without the burden of this condition. We must have celebrated for months.

We continued traveling right up until Jay was five. It was fascinating to watch him experience and embrace life all around the world. He's played with kids of all colors and races in various communities, got into a water fight at the Songkran festival in Thailand and watched the candles float up in the sky. When he visited my office in the Philippines, everyone called him "the little boss."

Traveling with Jay gave us great family times. Dad loved bonding with him around Europe. Every time we visited my favorite spa in Koh Samui, everybody knew who we were. The waitresses there were always keen to look after Jay. In the places we frequently visited, we were treated like family.

I have a portrait of Jay and me on my office wall. We're walking on a road in the Pyrenees Mountains between Spain and France. With our backs to the camera, we're facing the future. It's symbolic for me because it's a reminder to keep going—keep going on adventures and keep exploring the wonderful big world out there. Our nomadic life has been, and is, amazing.

CHAPTER 10

I Made It: The Paradox of Success and Failure

In its first four years, Remote Staff was 100 percent remote, with no office, and team members working from all over the Philippines. This setup allowed me to have a home in Sydney, visit the Philippines regularly and travel widely. But the remote nature of the workforce and the company's rapid growth presented challenges around onboarding new staff. Our systems and processes were not optimized, and all our best performers were promoted to management roles without getting any management training and without making the new management roles clear to them. We struggled to keep up with the volume and struggled to maintain our quality of work. But when I divided the business into departments to better handle the volume, they developed into silos, with a lack of communication between them.

Many of my business friends had expressed the view that you're not a real business until you have an office, and I was curious to see if the business would perform better with an office-based team. In December 2011 I located an office space in Makati, a business district in Manila that's conveniently located near lots of lively areas, shopping centers, hotels, and the airport. We retained some of the founding team members who lived close enough to the new office but had to let go of most of those who worked from other parts of the country.

We set about hiring a new, office-based team. This experience was like rebuilding a four-year-old business from the ground up. I thought I knew every role and function in the business, and that I just needed to hire suitable people and seat them together. But I underestimated just how difficult this would be. With my founding remote team, I'd experienced no politics, but within the new office-based team there were a lot of underlying power struggles. The same departmental silos formed once more. Nobody knew what anyone else was doing in the team or how their work played a role in the bigger scheme of things. And those original team members still working remotely started feeling like second-rate citizens.

After four months setting up the office team, Rica and I flew back to Sydney to see how we went managing the business remotely. But things just were not the same as they'd been with an all-remote team. The business was still growing despite all this disorder because the offshore industry was booming around the world. But we'd gone from having an empowered, dynamic culture to having a bad company culture. It was enormously frustrating.

For most of 2012, I was establishing new management teams to help get the various departments and the business to perform efficiently. Every month I'd spend a few weeks in Manila. I had my work cut out for me: Operations and teams were dysfunctional; people were in the wrong jobs; systems were falling apart, and company processes were being misunderstood. And my strengths do not lie in operation. During this time Rica, who is more skilled in operations, could not fly as frequently as me. She stepped out of operations to focus on running the accounting and IT departments.

By the start of 2013, Rica had had enough and wanted to leave the business. She was finding the new team difficult to work with and was still unhappy that the founding members had been terminated. She also wanted to spread her own wings and to give the entrepreneurial journey a go for herself by starting her own business.

Her idea was to build a remittance business to help OFWs (overseas Filipino workers) in Australia, mostly nannies, nurses, engineers, and hospitality personnel. Filipino workers remit their AUD income and savings over to the Philippines in pesos to support their families.

Remitting via banks was very costly, and she thought she could provide a more competitive forex solution for OFWs than the banks.

It took me almost a year to find a manager to replace Rica. By the end of December 2013, Rica left the Remote Staff business to start her new remittance business. Over the next four years, Rica grew the company from zero to $100 million in revenue, leading a team of thirty—all while only working part-time and being a home-schooling mum and wife.

Leaving the business challenges behind, I returned to Sydney for my fortieth birthday in March 2013. I went to an Indian restaurant with friends in Sydney and the next day flew to India. The main purpose of the trip was to go back to the ashram in the south of India that I'd experienced back in 2006. I wanted to meditate and recapture the magic of the place. That's all I wanted for my birthday.

The last time I was there, I didn't have wealth, a wife, a child or even a house, so it was easy to practice the Buddhist philosophy of nonattachment. I thought it would be interesting to see what impact those teachings had on me at this very different phase in my life.

When I went back there, I thought I'd be able to touch my inner essence as I had previously, but it didn't happen. Unfortunately, I found it difficult to meditate because they had a good Internet connection available for my phone even though the meditation places didn't allow anything digital.

The ashram building is a square and the long, thin rooms are on these different levels, with common showers. Each room had a wardrobe, a desk and chair and a window. A very simple room with a beautiful view. I was there to have my quiet time and reflect, but I was always tempted to get my phone and computer out. No matter how softly I was typing on the keyboard, someone would knock on my door.

"We still hear you."

They knew I was working. They felt my vibe. It was fascinating. They got me every time I opened my laptop. I was using my phone as a hotspot, so I wasn't on their network. But they *knew*. But the temptation of getting online was too much to resist. I couldn't help but engage my desire to work rather than clear my mind and meditate.

I was a busy person now, with a family and a thriving business, and I found it almost impossible to immerse myself in silence. I still enjoyed meditation, but I had too much going on. I wondered what the hell I was doing there. I was supposed to be there for a minimum of fourteen days, but on the seventh day, I left.

It was only five dollars a day to stay at the ashram, but I gave them a few thousand dollars instead. I wanted to support them and show my appreciation for what they had taught me before. I literally bowed out. I asked myself, where would I rather be right now? Koh Samui! So, I flew to Thailand and went to the health resort. I arrived on the day of Songkran, the water festival. People were throwing water and having fun, and I loved being a part of it.

All I can say is that the Chris in India back in 2006 at the age of thirty-three was very different from the Chris seven years later who returned to India on his fortieth birthday.

Back in the Philippines, I was at a loss about how I could get the business moving forward. And instead of intensifying my efforts with Remote Staff, at a time when the offshore staffing industry was rapidly growing, I turned my attention to another enterprise. I was interested in investing in real estate around Manila but had learned that it's tricky to make investment decisions there because it was almost impossible to determine the true value of real estate. There weren't any dedicated real estate portals to help people make informed buying decisions, except for a lot of general classified websites that sold jewelry, cats and dogs, and a whole variety of products. There wasn't a customized real estate property site similar to what we have in Australia, such as realestate.com.au (or Zellow.com in the US), which is a sophisticated tool for sellers, investors and homebuyers alike.

Since I was running a technology company managing local Filipino people, with the marketing know-how, a unique vision and an idea of the landscape and the market, as well as surplus cash to invest in a new business, I had the means to establish a real estate portal. And so, two months after Rica had left Remote Staff, in February 2014, realestate.ph was born.

Starting the real estate portal and running Remote Staff at the same time meant that I needed to be based in the Philippines. So, I bought an apartment and relocated my family there for a year. It was a new beginning, and more importantly, an all-out commitment not just of my time but of my family and my life. I enrolled my son in a school in the Philippines. The decision was all-consuming and very exciting.

Unfortunately, I wasn't the only one who could see that gap in the Philippines. Two global competitors with millions of dollars to burn were also developing real estate portals around the world. They were OLX (owned by Naspers) and Lamudi (owned by Rocket Internet Berlin). These two big competitors started developing portals at the same time as I did and were driving the Philippines market and educating the whole country about the value of a customized real estate portal. I simply followed suit.

I accomplished what they were doing for a fraction of the price and with a fraction of the team. We were generating nine thousand inquiries each month and had over two hundred thousand visitors to the website. At one point, we had fourteen thousand brokers listing their properties on the website and for a period of six months we had 105,000 real estate listings in the country. These numbers were impressive but were generated by paid advertising. To be a real estate online market center, we needed organic traffic to grow, and people who used the website once to return. After one year, this was finally occurring, and it was becoming a viable real estate online portal.

Things were looking promising, but I wasn't aware of just how different the real estate industry in the Philippines was. Australia is a society that is more used to living by rules, and standardizing its processes, legislation, and conduct. These layers of governance make it safe for the consumer to interact with agents and get service of value. That wasn't evident in the Philippines, where a lot of agents only worked on a commission basis and were not full-time in the industry. There was no governing body or structure to standardize the behavior, ethics and practice of real estate agents at the time. And yet customers were relying on these agents to help them make important decisions regarding an expensive lifetime investment.

We had to work hard with the market, as did my competitors, to educate these agents on how to be more professional, for example, by giving the official address of the properties they listed with us. If we were given a proper, dedicated address, we could pin it on a map and offer a search that would yield more refined, relevant results for our consumers. Offering results that were more targeted meant that the inquiries we received were more qualified and appropriate.

One of the reasons real estate agents didn't advertise property locations was that they were worried about other agents stealing their listings. We also had to fight to convince them to take proper photos of the actual houses instead of walls. At one point, we had a compliance team of eighty people, mostly interns, who would call the agents to remind them to give more detailed information and basically "clean up" the listings. We did this to remove non-professional behavior among the agents, but more so to give our consumers a more refined user experience, with accurate, relevant data to determine value and interest—the kind of information that would empower them to make an independent decision on which properties to invest in quickly and efficiently. That's what I thought a functional real estate portal should offer its consumers.

One valuable lesson I learned was that the real estate market in the Philippines was pessimistic. Many people had been taken advantage of and were suspicious of people who wanted to help. They'd say, "What's the catch?" You had to prove yourself to gain their trust.

Real estate agencies feared that realestate.ph or the other new portals might steal their business, an attitude I found surprising. We assured them, saying, "We don't want a cut; we don't want to split your commission. We want to provide you with a qualified inquiry that can lead to a sale, and then we want advertising revenue."

The plan was to earn revenue through paid advertising on the site, which is how I understood the industry to work. Who wouldn't want to pay for advertising if it generated sales? I was trying to apply the law of reciprocity—when you contribute, there is a natural desire for the recipient to contribute something back. Our advertising rates were cheaper than our competitors' rates and I was selling at a price that didn't even make financial sense. I just wanted to get a reaction from the market that acknowledged my contribution, and the commitment that they would be willing to part with their money for this service.

My business model was designed to serve general consumers, but our revenue was supposed to come from the real estate industry. Much energy and effort had to be invested to generate sales leads for the agents.

Delivering a service for free and then intentionally restricting it until somebody pays you to lift the restriction was a new way of earning revenue for me. I understood business to be a vehicle for service and adding value to other people's lives, but the real estate portal industry was doing this in a different way. In the end, people were more than happy to use us for free and took full advantage of us as long as they could.

I'm a fighter and I'm game to take on massive challenges, but with realestate.ph, I bit off more than I could chew. Looking back, it's easy to say that I should have been more careful and aware of my limits. I wasn't prepared for what could have gone wrong. I wasn't prepared for how vastly different the real estate industry was in the Philippines compared to Australia.

My initial thinking was to give it one year, invest half a million and see how things went. After a year, progress seemed promising, so I continued putting money into the real estate portal business. We did succeed at becoming a portal and generating a lot of inquiries. At one point we had the most listings in the country. Everything pointed to a rewarding result, except commercially it wasn't making sense. The commercial realization just never happened.

Frequently flying between Manila and Sydney, I returned in February 2016 back to Sydney for one of my regular check-ups for my Von Hippel-Lindau syndrome. The news was bad. The doctors found two tumors in the back of the cerebellum.

I went to see the neurosurgeon who had operated on me in 2005. He proposed to take out one tumor at a time to minimize possible complications. That would mean two serious operations. I decided to get another opinion about this, to see if I could find a surgeon who could remove both at once. Rica suggested that I consult a highly respected neurosurgeon she'd heard about. He told me he could take out both tumors in the one operation. I had confidence in the new surgeon's manner and approach and decided to go ahead with the plan to operate early September 2016. But I hadn't fully appreciated the potential complications.

Whatever form the surgery was going to take, it was clearly time for me to get out of the real estate portal business. It wasn't something I had to think about. It was instant. I had to have serious surgery, and it looked like I would face challenges after it. As soon as I made the decision to wind the realestate.ph business down, a large weight was lifted from my shoulders.

I incurred big financial losses and lost two and a half years of my life at realestate.ph. In the past, I've also experienced losses from business failures, which have cost me more than many Harvard degrees. The price I paid for my business lessons was phenomenal, but it was the price I was willing to pay to have no regrets in life.

The opportunity cost of doing the realestate.ph business was that I lost momentum with remotestaff.com. I could have invested all that money into the Remote Staff business and grown my money exponentially.

A lot came together with the realestate.ph business: the lure of the timing, the market conditions, the possibility of owning such a large company, and my desire to start something new in a whole new industry, playing in a bigger league.

One of the lessons that I learned from the experience was that business has to both serve a purpose and also service your own interests. It has to serve your life. You can't serve others unless you're being served. Otherwise, there's too much friction. And too much friction prevents you from tapping into the greater power out there. The greater power is not a little stream; it's a torrent of abundance!

In my first business, Industry Outplacement, I succeeded financially but still felt the paradox of success and failure because I didn't like what I was doing. With realestate.ph, I loved what I was doing but failed to successfully commercialize it.

Unlike failing with my Easylog business, after failing at the realestate.ph business, I did not have the luxury of having a period of recovery. I had a life-threatening issue to deal with, so there was no time for psychological recovery or to go through an emotional healing process.

I think one of the errors I made with realestate.ph was I thought it'd be a quicker path to money. I did not intend to do it long term. I thought of it as a build-and-sell asset. I was interested in the cause, but I was doing it for quick money, which is different from the Remote Staff business.

Despite this failure, it was great to be out of my comfort zone and personal boundaries, mostly the mindset thing. I embraced an unknown journey and tried to create a solution in the Philippines, such as help them become better informed. I was focused on the goal/vision of what I was trying to accomplish.

I enjoyed its perks, such as meeting new people and distracting me from dealing with Remote Staff-related problems I was not ready to face. I was procrastinating with Remote Staff because I didn't know what to do.

I learned a lot of important lessons in that business failure. Somewhere along the line, the lessons I learned from that entrepreneurial play would serve me in the future.

One of the lessons I learned from failing with the realestate. ph business was not to take things personally. I did not take it personally. I wasn't worried about not achieving success in the future. Unlike my first business failure with Easylog, which I did take personally and was worried I might never financially recover from my business loss.

It's when you do stuff like this that you learn what works for you. It became apparent that realestate.ph was not for me. So I shifted my focus to Remote Staff, wherein I was significantly motivated. Remote Staff was more in line with who I am.

One failure does not dictate your future. Sometimes, you will fail, but these experiences shape us. They won't necessarily define us. It will derail you but failure does not have to be a trap. You could really fall into this trap if you take it personally. It could take a while to get over it, and you could let your imagination run wild, and in my case, these experiences really did shape me.

We have to go through experiences like this to look into a mirror and be honest with ourselves. That being said, we can't be hard judges of ourselves during these times.

At the end of the day, there are risks to new adventures. What is failure but an opportunity to learn? When I am not caught up in the idea of success or failure, I am more focused on the journey and what I hope to accomplish. Success is never guaranteed, nor is failure. They're just outcomes. Every journey opens me up to more opportunities that are often more valuable than the successful outcome I'd originally hoped for.

Making a choice to try and making a choice not to try both require the same amount of energy, so why not make the choice to try?

Struggling financially all our lives is the price we pay for not going after our dreams. We find ourselves negotiating with people. "Can I make my payments in installments?" or "Can you waive the fifteen-dollar fee?" We're still trying, except that our finances become an all-consuming factor in our lives.

CHAPTER 11

Beginnings and Endings

Around the same time as my second brain diagnosis, Rica was trying to get pregnant. She really wanted a second child to complete the family unit. We'd been lucky with Jay—conceiving him naturally and with him not having the VHL condition.

She had three IVF attempts but each time the embryos all had my condition. Unlike Rica, I'd given up on the idea of IVF, but Rica was getting ready to undergo her fourth IVF process, and this was when she became pregnant naturally with our second child.

One day working from my office I felt an incredible pain in my chest. I said to Rica, "I'm just going to get a massage to relax." I lay down on my stomach to get a back massage, but the chest pain was unbearable, and I had to stop the massage. My heart was in physical pain.

I knew Dad was dying. I just knew. I hadn't felt this pain when I'd visited him in Melbourne a month earlier. I never wanted to believe that he was dying, but now I sensed it and it was breaking my heart, not just emotionally but physically too.

I was biding time, like everyone else, waiting to hear the news and fly back for his funeral, but I couldn't bear it anymore. I went to the office crying.

I was restless and couldn't think anymore. I knew I had to see him before he died. I called Rica from the office on a Thursday and said, "I'm not coming home. I have to see my dad." I went straight to the airport and flew back to Melbourne overnight.

When I saw Dad the following day it was overwhelming, but I did my best to hold back my tears. The next day, I couldn't hold back my emotions. I cried and cried. Mum and Petra could see that I was struggling and knew I needed to have a moment with Dad alone. They gave me Saturday morning to have some time with him.

I sat down next to his bed and grabbed his hand to help him sit up because he couldn't move. I couldn't understand the muffled sounds that he was trying to make. He was very sick.

When I rubbed his back to try to give him some relief, I felt large lumps. I started trying to remove them because I thought they were something that got stuck from the bed, but when I removed the robe, I could see the tumors all over his body. There were lumps on his neck, chest and even his wrist. That's when I knew the extent of his cancer. I couldn't imagine the pain he had to endure in the end.

I lifted Dad gently to a sitting position on the side of the bed so he could look out of the window from his bed, and cradled him into my chest, feeling his heart close to mine. We tried to have a conversation, but Dad couldn't respond properly beyond mumbling some words.

"Hey look, Dad, it's a beautiful day outside. You haven't had a chance to see it all day. I'm just going to hold you so you can look outside."

In that moment, embracing my father, we had a heart-to-heart connection. Something happened, and I became so much more at peace with the thought of my father's passing. I had an appreciation of the cycle of life. He had held me in his arms when I came into this world, and I held him in my arms in the last few days of his life. My heart mended when I embraced my father.

Later that day, I took my mum and sister out for lunch to thank them for giving me one-on-one time with Dad. When we got back to the hospital to be with Dad, I asked the nurse, "How can you determine how much longer someone's got?"

The nurse explained that it was because of the way the body shuts down and how organs begin to fail. She said that doctors were fairly accurate when death was a day away, but they started to see the signs a week or two earlier.

"How long has my dad got?" I asked.

"A week or two at the most."

As a family, we all discussed Dad's situation and made the decision to stop the rejection tablets he was taking for the kidney transplant he'd had years ago. If he only had a week or two left, then why wait? We didn't want to see him suffer anymore.

We made the decision in the afternoon—Mum, Petra, and me—with Dad nodding his head and the nurses in the background nodding too. It wasn't as if he had a few years left; he only had weeks, so if anything, we stopped the medication about a week earlier so that he could pass away naturally.

The following day, Sunday, I was on a plane back to the Philippines to be with Rica and Jay. Well before knowing that my father was dying, I'd prebooked an expensive trip to Coron, Palawan, for our anniversary. A few days later, Dad called me. Rica, Jay and I were at the Fairmont Hotel in Makati having breakfast. The call was completely unexpected. I didn't know what to make of it, to be honest.

Dad said, "Hey, Chris, how are you doing?" He was talking as if he was normal. It was spooky.

We had a good conversation. I was confused.

"Thanks very much for coming to visit me. I love you very much, my son."

"I love you too, Dad." I'd already said my goodbye when I was over there and had even deleted Dad's number from my phone because I was letting him go.

Dad spoke to Rica and Jay, and it was very low-key and conversational. It was just a normal call in the middle of breakfast.

I hung up the phone, looked at Rica and shook my head, confused. "I could've sworn he was dying. Now here he is, calling me as though he's going to come see us next week or something!"

Rica shrugged her shoulders. "It's freaky, Chris. He sounded really good."

I knew his pain relief medication had had major side effects. They slurred his speech and slowed him down, making him a vegetable. When he stopped the antirejection drugs for his kidney, he also stopped the pain relief, and that's why he could talk to us as though he was in good health.

Dad said his real goodbyes to us in that phone call. The next day, April 20, he died at sixty-eight years of age.

Seeing Dad just before he died allowed my heart to heal. It was so nice that he knew I was there for him toward the end of his days. I felt that was more important than being there for his funeral. My immediate family didn't expect me to attend the funeral, but my surrounding family, friends and relatives were shocked that I wasn't there. They weren't aware that I'd spent time with Dad a few days before he passed away.

Thinking about my father, I realized how his life had been a warning for me in my younger years. I had seen how hard Dad had worked for Mr. Gjergja at ATCO, yet Dad wasn't driving the same fancy sports car that Mr. Gjergja was driving. Mr. Gjergja influenced me, in a *Rich Dad, Poor Dad* kind of way, to become an entrepreneur and not fall into the "comfort" trap of a life of just getting by.

My dad and Mr. Gjergja had a very good relationship. Mr. Gjergja was Dad's boss when they were working and a good friend when they were not working. As a matter of fact, he gave Dad a big chunk of money when he sold his business, and it was he who paid for the palliative care, the funeral and the wake when Dad died. My dad looked out for him, and he looked out for my dad, right to the end.

My preparation for my second brain operation

We came back to Australia from the Philippines to get ready for the operation. The day before my operation was Father's Day in Australia. Rica and I went to an expensive seafood restaurant we liked to go to for special occasions. We were both wondering what life was going to be like after the operation. I didn't want to worry her more than necessary—after all, she was eight months pregnant with our second child—so I deliberately downplayed what I'd have to go through to have the two tumors removed. We kept the conversation mainly around the baby's imminent arrival and how I hoped to be back on my feet properly before then.

In September 2016, five months after my father passed away, I walked into the hospital wearing my jeans and a shirt, without even a change of clothes in my bag. Despite my misgivings, I tried to stay positive, telling myself I'd be out in a few days, in time to help Rica prepare for the birth of our second child.

After a six-hour operation to remove the two brain tumors, I lay unconscious in intensive care for days. I vividly remember a sense of having a conversation with someone before I woke up four or five days after. I was in an empty, dark place—another time or dimension. No light, no physical expression, just a sense of being present in a black void. I was in an urgent conversation. A man I could not see but whose voice I heard from my left said, "If you don't return to your body, it's a permanent decision. You won't be able to return to life."

I felt my father's presence from my upper right. I don't recall his words, but he was distressed—like he was campaigning for me to live.

I made my choice: "Yeah, I'm going back."

Then I woke up. Everything was skewed. I was trying hard to make sense of what had happened to me. I couldn't breathe properly. I couldn't talk. When I opened my eyes, I saw double and my head spun. One eye had clear vision; the other was blurry. Whichever way my eyeballs went, my head would spin uncontrollably in that direction.

My right arm and leg felt like they were on fire, but I could partially move them. I couldn't move the left side. My left arm had no control; it was floppy and shaking. I felt unbearable pressure in my head.

Nobody could understand a word I was saying because I was stuttering. My lungs didn't work fully, and I couldn't breathe normally. Half my face didn't work. On top of all that, I was completely deaf in my right ear.

I screamed out, trying to ask what was going on. Someone came to check on me and was concerned to see my right eye was significantly dilated.

My mouth was parched. I remember saying I wanted water. In my mind I was communicating this clearly, but what came out was gibberish. I didn't know that the left side of my tongue wasn't working.

I eventually had to whisper for anyone to understand what I was saying. It was a real struggle to breathe and trying to speak wore me out.

I moved in and out of wakefulness, often overcome by sudden fatigue. I remember looking at the clock and wondering how I was going to get through the next ten minutes, let alone the next hour.

Rica arrived in the late afternoon—Rica, my life partner of ten years, who I'd build a successful business and a wonderful life with. Rica, the mother of my six-year-old son. Rica who was eight months pregnant. The plan had been for me to be out of hospital in a few days, in time to help her prepare for the birth of our second child. This outcome was a disaster. She heard screaming and wondered whether it was me. When she came in, she was horrified.

"I know this is alarming for you," the nurse told Rica. "He wants water, but we can't give it to him because he could choke." Rica sat with me, shocked at the state I was in. She asked to speak to the surgeon. Apparently, he had been trying to get in touch with her but had the wrong number. When Rica called the hospital earlier, she was told that I was OK and that I'd be in intensive care just for the day.

The surgery had not gone as expected. The two dangerous tumors had been removed from my cerebellum (the brain part responsible for sensory perception, motor control, balance and coordination) but when one of the tumors was touched, it had burst and bled in the brain. "It was very bloody," Rica was told. "We thought we were going to lose him. He's lucky to be alive."

When Rica came in the following morning, she was expecting that I'd be better. But they told her I'd been in the ICU all night and they were still observing me. The doctor told her that he was still worried. Scans showed that the brain swelling was not subsiding as they expected.

Throughout the day, other doctors came in and out to check on me. Later in the afternoon, one of them pulled Rica aside and said, "Look, we're not out of the woods yet. If the swelling doesn't stop, we'll have to go in for another operation to stop the swelling."

"Why?" Rica asked.

"The skull is very small, so if it continues to swell, it will affect the rest of his brain and he could die."

Rica couldn't believe what was happening.

On the fourth day after I awoke, I was finally moved out of ICU to my own room, but I still couldn't see or talk properly, or move my arms normally. I just slept the whole time as if I was in a coma.

It was three more days before Rica could understand what I was saying. She had to guess what I was asking for. I'd try to say one word, such as "water," and she would help me drink bottled water through a straw or feed me pureed food because I couldn't swallow properly. I couldn't do anything, not even go to the toilet. It took me a month before I could even wipe my own ass because I had very little control in my right arm and none in my left.

I argued with the doctors constantly, telling them that it was supposed to be an in-and-out process, that I shouldn't have had these massive side effects. I needed Rica to help me physically and mentally. I needed her badly. I was not in a good frame of mind.

"It's better for me to die," I told Rica. It was the first time that I reached the point of saying it was easier just to die than to feel such extreme suffering. How was I supposed to live the rest of my life? It was no way to live.

"No, Chris. That might be better for you, but not for me," she replied. "We'll get through this." Later, she said that she had to consciously stay positive; otherwise, we would have just pulled each other down. When I was at my lowest, she said, "Enough is enough," and brought me back up.

It looked as though Rica was living on adrenaline, but she insists she was living on love. She was there for me the whole time because she knew that I really needed her. It wasn't that I didn't trust the hospital system, but I couldn't do anything for myself and if I did manage to press a button for help, it would usually take them half an hour to respond.

The night I got moved to my own room, I had a screaming match with the nurse because she told Rica to go home. "Get me out of here. If my wife's not staying, I'm not staying," I screamed. Rica refused to go and lay down on the floor because they wouldn't give her a bed. There she was eight months pregnant!

On the second night, Rica slept on the floor again until some-one brought a bed in for her at 2 a.m. I think it finally sank in that they couldn't get rid of her. Rica was there 24-7, my advocate.

We understood that hospitals had regulations, but the fact was that I needed her. Having her by my side gave me comfort while I was going through this nightmare I'd woken up to. If she wasn't there, it wouldn't have taken much for me to completely lose it.

She didn't move from my side except to go to the bathroom or get food. I was in a private hospital, but it was understaffed. There were three shift changes in twenty-four hours, with three different nurses every day—not a good system. They often didn't know what other medications I was on. They didn't know I was on high blood pressure tablets, and sometimes they'd forget I had other things to watch out for. Rica watched out for me the whole time.

Rica never once appeared stressed. Later she told me, "I was focused on the fact that you were alive. Even though you were swearing at the doctors, I felt love for them because all I thought about was that they're keeping my husband alive."

She knew how angry I was, but believed it was good that both tumors had now been removed. The first neurosurgeon that we'd consulted had proposed to remove one tumor at a time, in separate operations, to minimize possible complications. But we had con-sulted another highly respected neurosurgeon, who said it could be done in one operation. Not wanting to undergo the knife to my brain twice if I didn't have to, I had chosen to go with that plan. But I hadn't fully grasped the risk.

"Who's to say these things wouldn't also have happened if the tumors had been removed one by one?" Rica said to me now. "We can only speculate. Who's to say the tumor wouldn't have burst anyway? Who's to say you wouldn't have died on that table?"

Rica was very practical, my rock. She viewed it as a process we had to go through, saying everything would be OK. She later said, "I coped because I focused on feeling grateful that you were alive. You have to strip it down to the basics of what's important to you as a person. Everything else is fluff."

Rica could see minuscule improvements daily. On the first day in my private room, I couldn't talk or walk but by the second day I could turn my head, and the following day I could swallow water. Rica was grateful she was there because otherwise she would have been more worried. I had to relearn so much—things people take for granted like picking up a cup and drinking water. You don't normally think about it, but if you watch a grown-up go through the process of relearning that, it can be a shock. It's not simple to hold a glass and put it in your mouth and then sip water after you've had a brain operation. You must break it down into the mechanics: reaching out to a glass, holding the glass steadily, putting the glass to your mouth and tilting the glass so you could drink from it. All those things had to be relearned. My road back was going to be long and hard.

Having Rica by my side was a gift from God and I'll be forever indebted to her for staying beside me the whole time. I thought I was going to die, and I didn't want to die alone. She was with me when I needed her the most. But one day I saw her cry. "I miss Jay." Not seeing our little boy for days was hard for her, even though we had family helping us.

In the couple of years leading up to the operation, I had been so busy running a new business in the Philippines that we hadn't spent as much time together as in our earlier years. I was a driven, high achiever who worked for three weeks in the Philippines and then had one week in Sydney with my family. I worked long hours, and Rica was busy with Jay. We hadn't had that one-on-one time for a long time, not since before we had Jay.

With the busyness of life, work and family, you forget that there's this life partner you have and whom you love. I loved spending time with my wife. It was so nice to enjoy Rica's company even though it was a very difficult time. We made the most of our time together and managed to have little pockets of fun. We joked about the nurses holding the urine bottle for me in the middle of the night and we laughed about my chocolate mousse addiction. In a diet of bland pureed food, it was a heavenly treat.

My mobility challenges have given me a lot of time to think about my theories of near-death experiences and how we all have a choice. No matter how bad it is, we all have a choice whether to live or to die. This choice is given to all of us, even if it's only a micro-second. It happens on some other level of awareness, not governed by our understanding of time.

Watching me recover from the operation hit home for Rica. I was no stranger to hospital stays and medical interventions, and Rica had accepted me years before when I told her that I had VHL but seeing me go through the brain operation and its terrible complications made her see the severity of our situation. She said she felt lucky that we'd had ten years without too many health issues. "I need to grow muscles to be able to lift you," she laughed.

Rica is strong, but I also know that she's had to contemplate a future without me in it and think about the future of our two children.

CHAPTER 12

The Long Road to Recovery

I was kept in hospital for a lot longer than I'd expected after the brain operation. Then the hospital wouldn't allow me to go straight home. They said it wasn't safe for me without all the proper care and equipment, such as the bed, walker and bathroom facilities needed for people with such severe disabilities. I reluctantly agreed to go to a rehabilitation center specializing in neurotherapy, though my feeling was that the whole thing was rushed. I felt like the hospital staff wanted to get me out of there as I was not an easy patient for them to deal with!

I still couldn't walk or even get up off the bed, so they put me on a stretcher. They strapped me in. My head was spinning each time they moved me. I was arguing and debating with them frequently. I was trying to raise my voice with half a working lung. They transferred me and Rica by ambulance. When we got to the rehab center at about 10 a.m., the receptionist said the room wasn't ready, and to wait in the lounge.

"How can we wait at the lounge? My husband is on a stretcher," Rica said, shaking her head. "We need a bed." I couldn't sit on a chair, hold myself up or even breathe properly. They didn't understand just how severe my symptoms were.

I lay on the stretcher in the lounge area. When the reception staff realized how bad my condition was, they knew they couldn't keep me in the waiting room and took me to a temporary room with another patient in it. He was very old and living with dementia. When we got to the room, I asked a nurse to remove the stitches in my head because they were supposed to have been removed at the hospital before I left. My speech was still slurred from the operation and the male nurse looked at me as if I had dementia too. He completely ignored my instruction and wrapped more bandages on my head.

"Mate, you didn't remove the stitches," I yelled after him, but he walked off.

The rehabilitation center was designed for people with neurological issues, such as stroke victims. It was filled with elderly people. It was supposed to be a recovery center or a healing environment, but I felt that the staff showed zero care for their patients. I had Rica to help me but what about all the old people who were there alone? The whole place was depressing. I knew that if I stayed there, I'd become very stressed, and this would affect my recovery.

I pressed the buzzer for assistance. The nurse who'd put the bandage on my head came back in. "I'm buzzing you because I want to go home," I told him firmly.

"Yeah, all right," he said and then ignored me again.

Rica tried to talk to him about her staying with me, but he said, "That's not an option."

When he left, Rica whispered to me, "I'm not going to leave you, Chris."

For me, that was it. Even though I was still in bad shape, I could see that the place was derelict. There was a cleaner who appeared to be a very unstable individual as he was talking to himself. I remember thinking, I'm a wealthy man; I can afford my own cleaner, my own tea lady, my own rehabilitation therapists. Stuff this environment, I'm getting out of here. But because of my physical state, I wondered how I was going to get out. I could barely move.

"Rica, take me to someone who will listen."

When they finally put me in my own room, I asked Rica to show me around, even though it took a lot of energy to get out of bed, let alone go for a stroll on a heavy-duty walker. I was wobbly and slow and often out of breath. I could barely speak.

Rica said, "Chris, to your left is the garden. To your right is the coffee area. And we're now passing the nurses' area."

At that point, at the nurses' area, I told her to stop, and I started screaming my head off. "If my wife can't stay, then get me out of here. I need someone who can get me out of here, I'm not staying here." I shouted with my eyes closed because I still couldn't see.

The nurses stopped what they were doing and stared. I must have looked deranged—they may not have even understood what I had just said. When I finished screaming, one nurse asked, "Who are you?"

Rica emerged and said, "He's Chris Jankulovski from Room 9."

"Go back to your room. Someone will come to talk to you."

We went back to the room. Ten minutes later a psychologist came in.

Rica argued, "Why are they sending you? Chris doesn't need a psychologist. I want to talk to someone about getting him out of here." They really thought I was crazy. While the psychologist did an assessment of me, Rica went in search of the center director. "Look, this is not going to work. We have to get my husband out of here," she told him.

"It's the safest place for your husband to be," he insisted.

"It might be the best rehabilitation center in Sydney but it's not the best place for Chris," Rica argued. By this time, it was 2 p.m.

Rica kept arguing with the director, insisting that it was my decision, but he said, "No, your husband can't think properly. You're responsible for your husband. If he slipped, knocked his head, and died, it would be on you because you'd be going against medical advice."

I understood what they were saying. They were concerned about how a small woman like Rica could manage me, a bedbound ninety-kilogram man. At one point, I wondered whether it was a good idea. But I was horrified that they did not listen to my requests. I was the customer. Why argue with me? I was not used to being ignored and treated that way.

They would not release me unless Rica signed for me, taking full responsibility, which she did. Then we asked for an ambulance, and they said it would cost $1,000 and we'd have to wait until one became available.

They were obliged to take care of me, but I certainly wasn't feeling the "care." It was a scary situation to be in because I didn't have control of my own life. The doctors did. If Rica hadn't been there, they wouldn't have released me.

While we waited for the ambulance, Rica started calling companies and checking websites to get hospital beds, walking aids, a special seat for the toilet, shower, and everything that I may need delivered to our home.

Most of them said they couldn't get the things delivered until the next day, but Rica insisted that it was an emergency and we needed it urgently. She found one company that could bring everything within three hours while she was still negotiating to get me out of the center.

Rica arranged everything and was even able to find, by Googling the solutions from her phone, a physiotherapist, occupational therapist, and other rehab solutions that could provide home service. At 4 p.m. she asked the director where the ambulance was, and he said it would come but he didn't know when. "It could be at any time from now until midnight."

"What do you mean?" asked Rica. "There's no set time?"

I couldn't bear the thought of staying there for one more minute, let alone waiting all night.

"We can't assure you of anything because it's not an emergency. The ambulance is really for an emergency."

Rica got straight on her phone again to search for a private patient-transfer service because I couldn't sit in a chair at that stage; otherwise, we would have taken a taxi. I needed to lay flat. Finally, she found someone who could pick us up at 7 p.m., and for $300—much cheaper than the ambulance.

Rica went back to the director and canceled the ambulance. He was surprised that Rica even knew about patient-transfer options. At seven on the dot, the patient-transfer van arrived to finally take me home. I was so grateful. They had rescued me from my rehabilitation nightmare. They were my knights in shining armor.

Home at last! Two men got me out of the stretcher and onto a wheelchair so they could carry me to the second floor where our bedroom was. My head was spinning uncontrollably, I thought I would faint or throw up all the while strapped to a wheelchair. It was a strange feeling to be carried in a wheelchair to the second floor of my new home by two grown men. I will never forget that moment. A few weeks before my operation, we'd just moved into this new home, a 1930s art deco-style house that needed to be refurbished. So many things needed fixing or updating.

After being in the hospital for a week and a day in the rehabilitation center, Rica and I were so happy to be back home. We felt as though we had been lost on an island and were finally rescued. We felt free to do as we pleased, without doctors and hospital staff ordering us around. It had been traumatic for both of us.

Jay, who was six at the time, was delighted to have us back at home and we were overjoyed to be with him. At first, he was alarmed about the state I was in but after a few days he started to relax, climbing over my bed, and teasing me about my "defects."

For most of September 2016, I slept or had my eyes closed. I'd open them a few minutes at a time. I sometimes felt as though my head was spinning, whether my eyes were open or closed. When I did open my eyes, I had double vision. My sight was blurry in one eye while the other eye had perfect twenty-twenty vision, but with two images overlapping. On top of this, my eyes were very sensitive to light, so I kept the blinds shut.

Time felt painfully slow, and each day was difficult to endure. I obsessed over the challenges I was having to deal with, trying to think strategically about how the hell I was going to overcome them. When you are recovering from a broken leg or kidney operation, you still feel like yourself. You may be temporarily debilitated, but everything else is still functional. But after my brain operation, everything about me was nonfunctional—my vision, hearing, balance and whole-body movement.

There was no way I could think about the future at this point—there was nothing but the moment. It was taking every bit of my energy just to keep it together for my family, to get through each day and to survive.

On occasions I woke up in the horror-movie experience that was my body and panicked. I would need to go to the toilet, but my body wouldn't move. I'd think, what's going on here? It would take a couple of seconds for my mind to adjust to the new reality that my body was not able. That was tough then and still is now. Sometimes I go to move my hand and it doesn't work the way it used to. It takes time to adjust to the new normal.

As much as I was struggling, Rica enjoyed having me stay in one place for the first time in ten years. I'd never been in one place for more than three weeks. It took this absolute disaster for me to finally slow down. I used to squeeze as much as I could out of every hour, every moment, every day.

It was also quite convenient for Rica and me to have that downtime because she couldn't do much anyway with her pregnancy. When I started to slowly improve, her whole system collapsed. Her backside hurt, her hips locked, she got an eye infection, a sore throat, a cough—all very late in her pregnancy. I don't know how she did it.

She had a bit of fun because she was in total control of me, something I wasn't used to. She had to do everything for me, including dress me. One day I caught a glimpse of myself in the mirror and had to look twice. Rica had dressed me in green shorts and a pink T-shirt. "What the hell."

Three weeks after arriving home, I finally managed to get myself out of my upstairs bedroom using my heavy-duty walker and, with the help of my housekeeper and mother-in-law, down the staircase. We celebrated that occasion with a cake, though I could barely keep my eyes open with exhaustion. Jay stared in horror, because I was squinting and struggling with my face, and my speech was slurred. Still, it was my first big achievement since the brain operation. Sitting upright took so much energy. After a short while I asked for help to be brought back up to my room.

Rica, Jay, and I spent our time together talking, resting, and enjoying the beautiful views of Sydney from our balcony and bedroom window. That room was the center of my existence. My hospital bed was beside our own bed, where Rica slept. Sometimes, Rica would get me pastries and things from the outside world and my mum and sister came from Melbourne to stay with us too. Without the help of the housekeeper and the family, it would have been impossible for Rica to take care of me. My mother-in-law from the Philippines and my sisters-in-law who live in the area also came to help, which was wonderful.

Rica was having an elective cesarean, so we were talking about delaying the birth of our child for a week because I still couldn't shower on my own and I didn't feel comfortable with my mum or sister taking care of me.

I had to learn how to use my body all over again in a new way, and it was a slow process. The physiotherapist and the OT taught me how to get out of bed and use the heavy-duty walker, how to get to the shower and back to bed, and how to take care of every movement that I needed to make to look after myself. I started by getting out of bed and leaning my legs against the bed for a few seconds. Then I'd flop back down. That's how I started. First, holding on to something, then not holding on to something. Micro, micro steps.

The physio gave me a belt with two handles in the back so that he could hold me upright and help me swing my right leg in front of my left. If he wasn't holding me, I would have just dropped to the floor like a doll. He moved me around like I was a puppet, doing the same exercises over and over, so that my neural pathways would fire up and start forming some new signals. Soon, even though my hips were not strong, and I had little control, I was able to swing and flop my leg in front of me. I used my leg as if it was a walking stick and was able to regain balance. That was a major achievement.

My mobility challenge was so severe, especially on the left side of my body, that the smallest, simplest motion, such as an exercise the OT asked me to do—to pick up a small pencil lid cover and move it from the left side of the table to the right—was enough to tire me out for the best part of an hour.

The process of rewiring the brain was immense. My brain had to learn how to do everything again. It was phenomenal. Any movement I tried to make would knock me out. I was in a bad way for the first two months. I was mostly just bedbound and suffering from extreme fatigue—up by 7 a.m. and knocked out by 2 p.m. I had a one-hour therapy session with the OT and another hour with the physio, so I focused on just getting through the day and preserving enough energy to sustain the rehab. That was it. Nothing but the present.

It took time to accept what was happening to me. After the operation, I was upset and angry. However, I went through a realization that this had happened to me, and I couldn't reverse it; it was done. I'd had the operation and the tumors had been removed. To come to that conclusion took me months. Once I accepted the situation, I was able to go through the healing process. It was only at that moment I shifted my focus to what I could do and what I could control. I stopped wasting energy on the list of challenges and decided to make progress even if it was infinitesimal. That was transformative.

I learned a lot from the rehab, and it helped me greatly. I had to learn how to walk and move my hands in a different way. In the first six months (and up to two years) the brain spontaneously heals; however, after two years, the spontaneous healing slows down to a crawl. Gradual healing occurs with subtle improvements here and there. The brain is so rubbery and can mold and reshape itself. The more I used my body in different ways, the more the brain would learn how to rewire itself. If I just sat on a chair and did nothing, then it wouldn't create new neural pathways.

I never knew that just standing independently was such a miracle. I had no idea that one could spin like a roller coaster when lying in bed. I had no idea that two separate eyes had two separate visions and it was the brain that would merge them together to give you a sense of depth. It was a horrible experience.

Some nights I'd wake at three in the morning. Then, in the black of night and unable to move, or with my head spinning, I grieved. We all grieve in different ways and for me it was verbal. As something came up, I would speak it. Having Rica there to listen helped me go through that verbal grieving process. I thanked God for having her there. Rica was my anchor, there every step of the way, and helped me heal faster.

The other thing that shifted my mindset was the Rio Paralympics, which took place in September 2016. When I saw the ad for the games, with its "Yes I can" slogan, I watched it over and over. Here I was, obsessing over my limitations, and here were these athletes with their disabilities and challenges embracing life, pursuing their potential, and not settling with their limitations. However broken I was, the video of the "Yes I can" slogan inspired me to rebuild my life.

Flourish through adversity

The uncomfortable truth is that at some point in our lives, things will go wrong. We all may eventually face serious adversity, often at unexpected times. For me, the adversity was extreme: the aftermath of my brain surgery and the painful road to rehabilitation that I described in chapter 12. I had to accept my new reality and shift my focus to what I could do.

It is so easy to be swept up negativity when things go wrong in life. If you let things always effect you and you're always reacting to challenges, you will end up taking longer to overcome your challenges. Here are four powerful steps to help you build resilience so you don't get deterred when faced with challenges in your life.

Accept your reality

Even if you're not in a crisis or facing adversity, but are simply trying to improve your life, first be willing to see things as they are in today's reality—not your version of reality—to correctly interpret the situation you are in.

After you've acknowledged your current reality without your biases, the next step is the most significant one toward healing, or for progress to occur. You need to accept your current reality by:

1. Accepting what you cannot control first; and
2. Accepting responsibility for the outcomes.

For me, the first step is often the harder one. It took me two months just to accept the reality I was in after my brain operation. The moment I did, I shifted my focus from my overwhelming list of adversities to what I could control. Accepting my new reality empowered me to actively take on my adversities, one small step at a time.

Take time out; stop everything for a while

It takes time to recover from hardships and failures. Such moments often force us to stop. It is essential that we do stop everything during these times, so our minds can be fully aware and process what happened. This often involves a full mental review of everything we may hold as truth. You may question everything: your assumptions, your beliefs, your worldview. I call this moment a mental reboot. It takes a lot of mental energy as most of it happens unconsciously. Eventually, your consciousness will become aware of the inward changes you have made. It's a grounding experience.

During this time out you gain new self-knowledge and perspectives of what is important in your life and what really matters to you. Adversities can potentially make massive lifelong changes in all aspects of our lives, changes that are far greater than the adversity itself.

Shift your focus toward what you can do

The energy you spend complaining all day about your problems has no pay-off, no joy, no vitality. It's a limiting experience. That same energy could be spent on solving the problem. All you need to do is:

- Shift your focus away from the past and focus on what you can control today.
- Be resolved in exactly what you want.
- Look for possibilities or ways you can deal with the issue.
- Take small steps daily. Eventually you will surprise yourself with how far you can go.

Actively maintain hope

The future is unknown, so why assume the worst when you could choose to hope that the best is yet to come? It all comes down to the choice you make as to how you want to see things and what you want to believe in.

It takes courage and faith to hope that the best is yet to come when everything seems hopeless. But hope can give you the energy you need to take action. With more hope, you are more likely to do more. Hope, faith, gratitude and work—combined—can lead to miracles occurring.

When you choose to actively maintain hope, regardless of the outcome, you become more certain in yourself, in God or in the universe. Even if you are dying and your time is limited, maintaining hope with gratitude allows you to appreciate your remaining days.

Knowing that Rica would be occupied with caring for the baby, I was determined to fast-track my rehabilitation by removing my dependency on assistive equipment. I wanted to be able to get out of bed on my own, to have a shower on my own and to go to the toilet on my own. I had to. Sometimes it would take an hour with the rehab team just to practice walking down the stairs or learning how to get to the car or how to wipe my own bum. It was raw and basic. But we got there.

The big day arrived. On October 4, 2016, Rica was taken in to have a cesarean, with a nurse pushing her in a wheelchair. I was wheeled in alongside her in my own wheelchair. I had worked hard on my rehabilitation to be there for the birth of our baby. It was hard to believe that we had deliberately set the date for my operation to be one month before the baby was due, certain I'd be fully recovered by then.

Instead, I was squinting because of the double vision, and it was hard to focus because of the glare. Even in a wheelchair, my head was spinning, and I was on the verge of throwing up. But then our beautiful baby was born. It was amazing—the miracle of life itself and the awareness that here I was battling to stay alive, and yet life was carrying on in my newborn son. Life finds a way to carry on. I held him for a few moments, overwhelmed, and then I left. Trying to manage my emotions as well as the physical challenges was utterly exhausting. I went home and crashed.

In memory of my dad, we called our son Billy—just as I am named after Dad's father, who was a Chris. I wanted to be reminded of the love that Dad had for the family. All those differences we'd had in the past were irrelevant compared to the vastness of his love. I know there will come a time when I struggle to remember moments of his love, affection and the times that we had together, but naming my son after him will help keep the memory of his love alive.

All the work I did on my rehabilitation in the lead-up to Billy's birth gave me hope. I couldn't allow myself to be attached to an identity of suffering. My left arm still didn't work, my vision was bad, and my tongue felt strange. All this was true, but it didn't have to be my truth—it didn't have to define me.

A few weeks after Billy was born, I went for my first walk to a coffee shop on my own, just using a walking stick. It was half a kilometer away and normally took five minutes to walk, but that day it took me an hour to get there. It was a glorious sunny day, and I was so pleased with my progress.

The next day, Rica and I decided to go to a coffee shop at Bondi. This time I was on my mid-sized walker rather than my walking stick because I was so fatigued after the previous day's walk. Rica put the walker in her Mini Cooper. When we got there, we parked close to the café, and Rica helped me out of the car and into the walker. All eyes were on us as we entered. No one knew what to do, but I was smiling. We were regulars, so many people recognized us, but they didn't know what had happened to me.

Rica and I were laughing at the absurdity of the situation when our meals arrived. I picked up my fork and knife, and that's when I realized, I couldn't use cutlery as I had before. My hands were shaking uncontrollably when I was trying to cut the bread; it was going everywhere—on the table and the floor. But I had zero self-pity. Rica and I were loving it—celebrating, enjoying being alive.

When we were done, my wife helped me back into the car. She swung my legs in, and the circus was over.

It was an important moment for us because Rica and I often had breakfast dates, rather than dinner dates. So, to get to a coffee shop, despite my adversities, filled me with hope that I could return to some normality in life one day. That maybe I could travel again, work again, create again—even start to pursue my full potential again.

CHAPTER 13

An Unstoppable Attitude in the Face of a New Adversity

A year after my brain operation, can you believe I had another major health setback? The results of a kidney test came back, and they weren't good. I was nursing 2 kidney tumors but out of nowhere, a total of six cancerous tumors were growing at a faster rate. After fighting so much just to get back on my feet after my brain operation, I had to now confront my mortality once again.

Having VHL meant that I was always going to have cysts and tumors.

But being bedbound for months as a result of my brain operation had created a toxic environment in my body. Some of my kidney tumors outgrew the safe size and now I was in danger of having cancer spread all over my body.

I contacted the trusted kidney specialist who had performed an operation on my left kidney back in 2008.

"Chris, we need to act straightaway," he said after reviewing my results. "We're going to do a similar operation to the one you had on your left kidney before. We'll be cutting you in the same place, but this time I'd like to use robotic surgery because it will cut off your tumors quickly and more efficiently."

He explained that to remove the tumors from the kidney, he would need to block the blood flow. Blocking the blood flow puts a lot of strain and pressure on the kidney. "Sometimes, the kidney can be so stressed without blood flow it will cease to function, and it could kill the organ."

I nodded, understanding the severity of the situation.

"So, the goal is to remove the six tumors within fifteen minutes using robotic technology and to save as much of your remaining kidney as possible. The faster we can do it, the more conducive it will be for your kidney to be revitalized and continue functioning. Are you OK with that?"

"Yes. What are my odds?"

"Chris, 90 percent of your healing recovery will occur in the first eight days after your operation if all goes well."

I had no choice but to go ahead with the operation.

I contemplated the situation for weeks. I just survived a brain operation and eight months of rehab to walk again. Now I had to confront the possibilities of having my remaining kidney dying after the operation or my kidney not functioning normally and being on dialysis forever, or having my cancer spread.

I was facing a grim future. While I was continuing with my rehab in the pool, I started listening to Kesha's song "Praying." It's a stirring song about going through hell and learning how to fight, and it connected with me, helping me see for the first time just how strong I'd become after all my health challenges. The song helped me find a strength I didn't know I had. The lyrics of the song were like me having a conversation with God.

It was because of this song that I dared to hope that the best is yet to come during the darkest period in my life.

So, on October 10, 2017, I had a second operation on my left kidney. I didn't know if after the operation I would be battling cancer, or whether I would even have a functional kidney.

My remaining kidney, now only half its original size after the operation, couldn't filter my blood properly. My creatinine level was at a dangerously high level of 590. A creatinine level of 600 represents a dead kidney, while a normal person with two healthy kidneys has an average creatinine level of 100. Five days later, on October 15, my creatinine level was at mid 500, only a four percent improvement over the previous five-day result. Things were not looking good, which was really concerning considering that I was halfway through my healing period.

That night in intensive care, I wasn't getting any decent sleep because the patients on either side of my bed were behaving irrationally. At four thirty in the morning, one of the male ICU nurses looked at me and said, "Chris, I can see you're not getting any sleep. The ICU is the quietest at this hour. You haven't had a proper shower and shave in six days. Do you want to take this opportunity to shave yourself and let me shower you?"

"No, I'll shower myself."

"No, you're too slow; I'll shower you. I'll do a better job. You just shave yourself, how's that?"

When I was finally showered and shaved, I felt like a new man. I was seated on a chair next to my bed, ready for breakfast.

A few hours later, a nurse I had never seen before, who I later learned was the head of the ICU department, came up to me and said, "Let's give you a break and move you into your own room." That surprised me. Such rooms in an ICU area were usually reserved for those who were trying to gain a few more minutes of survival. In my case, I felt like I was getting an upgrade from economy to business class.

A little later, my kidney surgeon came to visit me in my new private room and said, "I'm really worried about your kidney. It's not looking good. We're already past five days of the eight-day window where 90 percent of your recovery normally occurs. I don't know where you're going to get to in your recovery, but it doesn't look like we're going to achieve the result we all hoped for." The hope was to get my creatinine level down to 350 at least.

Right then and there, I realized I had to make a spiritual pledge to turn things around. I pledged, "Doctor, give me ten years and I will inspire millions." It was a spontaneous response in the moment because deep down I could sense that I had to spiritually turn things around. I'm trying to get the results I want, and I want more life. I want another ten years. I find this mind-body spiritual connection fascinating, it's surprisingly powerful. I was consciously making an effort with my mind to spiritually heal my kidney. Why not? I've seen the power; I believed if I could put my mind and heart into it, it could happen.

"No need for pledges. You don't need to bargain with me; it's my job to look after you. But your current results will get you five years. I think that's all you can achieve at this point."

"How about this—you focus on realistic results; I'll focus on miraculous results."

"The best scientific result is anything below 300," he said.

"How's 200? Would that get me ten years of life with my remaining kidney?"

"That would definitely be an outstanding result," he replied, smiling.

My doctor, who is a mathematical person, said, "Close to ten. You will most likely get seven years, but if you can look after yourself over those seven years, you might be able to stretch it to ten—if you achieve those outstanding creatinine results and if your VHL doesn't kick in with those aggressive tumor growths, you'll get your ten years."

"Done. We have a deal." So, we shook on it.

When I made that pledge on October 16, I felt a shift occur in me immediately that felt like overwhelming joy. I was celebrating right after. I was open to receiving a miracle and I knew right then that I would heal well from my operation. I intuitively recognized that things had just turned around with my health.

My blood test results got better and better. A few hours after my doctor's visit, the result came in at 490, a promising 15 percent improvement. Was it coincidence? Maybe. But I don't think so.

With only two more days left in the eight-day recovery window, I was getting a little worried. On October 17, my seventh day at the hospital, my results went to 425. This was a level that no longer put me at risk of being on dialysis, even though I still had many symptoms like swelling in my legs, and hot and cold flushes at night. I also still needed to be on a strict renal diet with such a creatinine level.

The next day, I was at 360. I left the special room at the ICU and was moved to my private room. My doctor came in and said, "You're doing much better."

"I'm not done yet, I'm still focused on achieving a miracle healing result," I said.

On Thursday, October 19, my creatinine level continued to go down, and was 320. And on the next day, I reached 295. On Saturday, October 21, three days past the eight-day recovery window, I was relieved to see that I was still making substantial progress with my kidney function.

After my kidney operation, I was in a heightened state of awareness. Friends and family who came to visit me at the hospital noticed that I didn't have the television on. I wasn't reading any books or playing with my phone. I was practicing silence and mindfulness.

I had to perform on a zen level with every physical movement I made, and be calculated and controlled, because my body could not move spontaneously. I had the option to press the help button for the nurses' assistance, but instead I always chose to move independently and safely on my own. I was also better able to observe my thoughts and feelings and capture visions and clues that appeared as momentary glimpses.

I recognized how incredibly hard the whole ICU team was performing. They were men and women from all walks of life and cultures, all innovative, seasoned, experienced nurses on top of their game. Every single one of them was responsible for every scenario that was occurring. It was amazing to see how they worked together as a team. What I loved most about them was that they were so observant about every detail. The care they gave me was exceptional. I saw it constantly and believe it was one of the major factors that facilitated my miraculous healing results.

The day I moved out of the ICU into my private room, I gave flowers to everyone working in the ICU and the kitchen staff, a total of more than seventy people. Thirty-three people were available to receive the flowers; the rest were on roster shifts and not available to receive the flowers within the week. I asked the florist to prepare the bouquets I gave away, which consisted of colorful gerberas and anemones because I wanted to celebrate their care.

The head nurse invited the marketing manager of the hospital to take photos of the gift-giving occasion. The marketing manager said that in all the twenty-four years she had worked with the hospital, she had never witnessed a thank you of this magnitude before.

My creatinine level was now at 265. My doctor was delighted with the results and discharged me from the hospital a few days earlier than expected.

On October 25, I had another blood test done by my local GP and got the creatinine result to 215. Then on November 3, another blood test came in at 180. By early 2017 my results finally tapered off at 125.

With a creatinine level in the low hundreds, I'm doing better than both I and the doctor had hoped for, considering I'm only on half a kidney and performing not too far off from somebody with two kidneys. My kidney surgeon, nephrologist, local GP and dietitian all think I'm superhuman!

I'd entrusted my kidney surgeon with my life on two occasions a decade apart. Both operations were successful, ultimately allowing me to gain more quality time on this earth. I remembered the pledge I'd made to my doctor a decade earlier, which was to employ thousands, even though at that time I didn't employ anybody. A few months after my February 2008 kidney operation, I'd gone full-time at Remote Staff, which I had started the previous year, and ten years later, it employed eight thousand people. I lived up to my pledge.

My recent promise to my surgeon was to inspire millions and as a token of appreciation I wanted to do something special for him. From my private hospital room, I called an art gallery owner at The Rocks in Sydney from whom I'd bought artwork in the past. He was a lovely man. I asked him to help me figure out what I could give a doctor who could buy whatever he wanted.

"Why don't you commission an artist to paint something for you?" he suggested.

I thought that was a brilliant idea, so I commissioned an artist recommended by the gallery owner to paint a story I summarized in a title called *Worthy*. The story was about my doctor giving me extra time that I wanted to be worthy of.

Almost one month after my operation, I received both paintings. The one he painted for me was titled *The Tree of Life*, and the painting for my doctor, which I loved even more, was titled *Worthy, Trust and Hope*.

The painting for my doctor featured a small human figure reaching out for many moons in the sky while standing on top of an elephant, which was on top of another elephant. The artist often put many moons in his artwork to represent the passing of time, and an elephant was added here to symbolize knowledge and ultimate trust. He put the two elephants on top of each other because I'd had two operations entrusting my life to the same doctor. The human figure—representing me on the shoulders of something powerful—is reaching for one of the moons, signifying my desire for more time on this earth.

I felt spiritually obliged to accomplish this new pledge and maintain my old pledge. Surely my life could count and be worthy of all these second chances that I've been given. I'm glad I changed my attitude about my health adversities in 2005, when I looked to the sky and made my original pledge to God by choosing to no longer be disempowered by my condition and to choose living an empowered life. If I hadn't made that original pledge back then, I don't think I would have been strong enough to survive the many other adversities I have had to overcome.

This strong attitude of mine has taken decades to develop. I've gone through eight near-death experiences. I've survived operations to remove not just one but multiple tumors from my body at once. I'm not new to adversity and I've had time to handle it better than most people. I have long recognized that gratitude is the foundation for healing, preventing the downward spiral into destructive personal psychology that prevents healing from occurring.

Somebody confronting a major health adversity for the first time may find it hard to see that it's possible to attain such an empowered attitude in such circumstances. A fellow patient in the ICU ward went through the same kidney operation as I did but to remove one tumor. I was there to have six removed.

"Just because you have this great attitude doesn't mean this impacts your health," he said. "There's no scientific proof that it does."

"Correct," I replied. "There's no scientific proof that this positive attitude is going to do anything for my health. But I'd rather have a strong mind at times like this. If there's hope that such things could offer healing, then I'd rather have the faith that keeping a strong mind can improve my odds of better healing."

The more you are in control of yourself, regardless of whatever adversity you face, the more aligned you become with your true intentions. You will start believing that your future is something to keep looking forward to.

These days, my doctor uses me as a case study in his lectures. He shows his students photos of the six kidney tumors he removed and tells them about my current kidney function results—and he shows them the painting I gave him.

Accepting reality and shifting my focus to what I could do took time and became another major life lesson for me.

When I shifted my focus to what I *could* do, I no longer judged my situation. I didn't care anymore about the list of disabilities I had. From then on, I focused on what I could do, with whatever conscious effort or whatever limited awake period I had. I was delighted by the empowering feeling of focusing on what I *can* control. It brought me to the point where, suddenly, it didn't matter what had happened to me; I was just grateful to see my family and grateful to still be able to apply myself and try to get back on my feet. I had turned the corner. For now.

CHAPTER 14

Getting Back to Full Health

After the near-fatal brain operation and the kidney operation, I was determined to do everything I could to increase my chances of staying well. My focus was on maintaining my fitness and improving my eating habits.

While I'd already kicked my other habits from the past, like smoking and drinking, my diet required a new approach. I'd gone cold turkey with cigarettes and alcohol, but I couldn't do that with food. I needed to eat. I thought becoming a vegetarian would be enough to improve my health, but it wasn't because I ate a lot more carbs in the form of noodles, pasta, and bread.

I finally had to get serious about my diet when I became diabetic in June 2017, which happened because of being bedbound for months after the brain operation, though my ten-kilo weight fluctuations over the previous decade couldn't have helped. I must have been prediabetic.

Taking control of my eating habits required much more than a positive attitude or willpower. I started working with a dietitian, an endocrinologist, and my GP, and read up on a lot of information to better understand diabetes.

The dietitian helped me to understand which foods I should eat and which I should avoid, such as keeping carbs to a minimum and avoiding sugar as much as possible. It was a process of making wise eating decisions and switching to healthier alternatives. I became more aware of when I was full and removed extra food from my plate, controlling portion size. I understood my emotional response to food and learned to distinguish between the short-term pleasure I felt when eating unhealthy options and the satisfaction I got from making good choices.

I learned about my body's physical response to the food I ate by using a glucose monitoring device linked to a phone app to measure food responses. It helped me make wiser choices. For example, I learned I could enjoy a whole wheat spelt-base pizza from a local pizza shop. I tested my reaction using the device and my blood sugar levels did not spike. That was good news!

On my own, I was able to make a 30 percent improvement in my glucose levels, but with the glucose monitoring device and the help of the dietitian, I was able to make a 60 percent improvement in reducing my glucose levels from the highs of 13 to 14, down to the normal HbA1c level of 5.6.

Within six months, I managed my diabetes. My endocrinologist told me he only had a few patients every year who successfully do this through their diet. He then asked me, "Don't you feel like you're missing out on a lot of things in life?" I thought it was an odd question because from my perspective, I get to be alive longer by eating healthy food. If I followed the general advice and just took pills for my diabetes without making those other changes, it would not be addressing the cause. Within a decade, my pancreas would stop producing insulin. My medication dosage would increase to a point where I would have to live on insulin injections. By getting on top of my eating habits, I would be able to sustain my pancreas function and maintain a healthy blood sugar level for life.

I used to have a c'est la vie attitude toward life, thinking whatever will be will be. Eight out of ten people I talk to say that since life is short, they might as well eat, drink, smoke and do whatever they want. Instead of addressing the cause of an illness, they'd rather just deal with the symptoms. But if I only had three more months to live, my attitude would not be c'est la vie these days: I'd rather enjoy those last three months in good health rather than decline toward the inevitable.

It took me time to recognize that responsibility for my own health and well-being is 100 percent up to me. Sometimes I don't eat well, but at the end of the day, it's an averages game, and I recognize that I'll get better results by being consistent with healthier options over the long term.

As well as working on my diet, I continuously work to use my left arm and left leg in the gym. There was nothing wrong physically with my left arm or leg, it was just that the electrical impulses were not firing, and the normal patterns were no longer in place.

The connection between the right and left hemispheres of my brain had been severed during the operation, cutting the electrical pathways in the part of the brain associated with mobility.

As I had mentioned earlier, I would never forget my attempt to use my left arm with the help of an occupational therapist after my brain operation in 2016. To do that for the first time in that kind of situation knocked me out so hard. I rolled over and basically said, "I need a moment." I was knocked out for thirty minutes.

The occupational therapist said to me, "You just formed a new connection in your brain and that is equivalent to a new paradigm shift. You see, your mind is not hardwired, and it can change, but it takes that much mental energy to change the electrical structure of your brain. The brain is a cellular infrastructure that, with enough repetition and use over time, forms electrical pathways. These pathways are like bridges and highways. But in your brain, these bridges and highways were broken, and therefore you could no longer use them. Instead, you must take the backroads when trying to perform even a basic movement. Over time, you'll be able to form new bridges and highways, but until that time you must take a much longer route, expending a lot more energy."

This explanation helped me a lot. I understood why it required such concentration to perform a basic movement, why I experienced fatigue sooner and why my movements were not as accurate. Every time I want to change something, such as create a new habit or get rid of one, I am reminded of that experience. I remember the amount of energy it takes, and the amount of effort needed to form new connections in my brain.

Over 2017 I continued my rehabilitation and was observing my newborn son, Billy, who at the time was learning how to walk and move his body. My movement and capabilities on my left side were progressing at the same speed as my newborn son. Our neurological pathways were forming at the same time at the same pace. Then he overtook me at three years old. The takeaway here is that neurological pathways and change takes time but change can happen.

Putting in the work with the OT and seeing my son develop helped me understand that our brain and minds are just a sponge of electrical pathways and patterns. I didn't know the word *neuroplasticity* at the time, but I've since learned that one can shape one's mind if one chooses to do so consciously. Electrical pathways in the brain have been developing since we were born, shaping our experience in the world—and these electrical patterns can be changed at will.

This started me thinking ... if the mind is a series of electrical patterns and you put in the work, you *can* change your mind— you're thinking, habits, beliefs, outlook—you can change it all. To do so is very powerful and courageous. Of course, genetics and behavioral tendencies also come into play, but there's so much we *can* change if we're willing to do the work.

Jay, my older son, is a carbon copy of me physiologically. He looks just like I did at his age, and it's uncanny how he responds and behaves just like me. In him, I can see the biological impact on how we think and behave the way we do. In Billy, I was able to see our physical abilities improve at the same speed, and therefore got to see firsthand how long it takes to form new neural pathways.

Everything I learned when I attended Tony Robbins's seminars around neurolinguistic programming finally connected for me during my rehabilitation. Through it all, I've gained a profound insight into how we can apply ourselves, challenge ourselves and, ultimately, change ourselves. I was learning about multiple aspects of well-being—my mind, emotions, mental state, the physical side of things, my diet—and my ability to reprogram my mindset. This is another of those big life lessons for me.

Understand the most powerful tool we have, our brain: How to Form new Thinking Patterns.

Your mindset is automatically formed overtime, it determines your general behavior, attitude, and outlook on how you see the world around you.. See it as your internal software operating system. When you can change your mindset, you can shape the way you think, change how you see things around you and transform your behaviors and outlook on life.

Our brains are uniquely created by the formation of synapses. By synapses I mean brain patterns. When you think, feel, or do anything for long enough, the brain patterns form as new electrical brain structures. However, our thoughts are just brain patterns formed over time; they are not hardwired. If you are willing to, you can change your brain patterns.

Change mostly happens via your unconscious. Your unconscious brain activity is huge and processes a lot of information automat- ically—beyond your control or awareness. Your consciousness only becomes aware of information if it is:

- Personally meaningful for you; or
- Aligned with your values and goals.

So, it's very important to know your own values and to write down your goals. Your consciousness has limited brain activity and limited memory and can only focus on what it is aware of.

To structurally change your mindset is simple, but it is not easy, for the following reasons:

1. A mindset change requires a lot more energy than we might realize.
2. Our brain tries to conserve energy whenever possible and is most comfortable doing nothing.
3. A perception that change is too hard to do will cause you to avoid it.
4. The more certain brain activities occur, the stronger your habits get, and the harder they are to change.
5. Change doesn't happen instantly, just by doing something once.
6. Understanding something isn't enough to create change.

To actively modify our unconscious mind to form new thinking patterns, follow these steps to increase awareness:

1. Slow down and practice mindfulness so you can pay attention to your thoughts without getting triggered by them. This way you can begin the process of self-reflection and reassessment of your mindset.
2. Note down any undesirable thought and observe any emotions that might be driving this.
3. Get certainty by educating yourself to gain a wider perspective on your undesirable thought.
4. Next time you notice the undesirable thought come up, challenge yourself: interrupt the thought and replace it with your new, educated understanding. Eventually your unconscious mind will remember your new views.

Practice your new thoughts over a period, to reinforce new patterns that drive your actions, habits, thoughts and behaviors. Eventually your old thoughts will drop away.

In August 2017, four months after I stopped using a walking stick, in consultation with my physio, I joined a gym and engaged a personal trainer. They couldn't believe I had been using a walking stick to get around until recently, let alone that I'd been bedbound a year ago, unable to walk at all without help. I was working on increasing muscle mass and strength because I'd lost 25 percent muscle mass on the left side of my body.

Some of the rehabilitation exercises I was doing with the physio to strengthen the left side of my body were one-legged balance exercises and left-arm movements. My gym instructor and I applied those exercises and movements in the gym with some weights added. It was a continuation of my rehab, and I still do it today. I am committed to the gym for life.

At home in my own living environment in Sydney, it was hard to notice dramatic improvements in my progress. Sure, I noticed a bit here and there, but I couldn't quite tell how far I'd come. It was when I returned to a place where I hadn't been for a time that I really had the chance to notice the changes—like when I went to Osaka three times, a year apart.

Not long after I started working out at the gym, I went on my first business trip a year after the brain operation. I bought a foldable, lightweight carbon walking stick that fitted in my back pocket. Finally, I could ditch the big brown grandpa walking stick

I'd been using until then. It gave me the confidence to walk around more without support, as I could just grab the stick from my back pocket whenever I needed it. I felt like a superhuman as I made my way around Osaka using that funky walking stick.

The following year in June 2018, I visited again. This time, I didn't need a walking stick, but my balance was still shaky. Crowds of people passing me by would throw me off my balance. I couldn't keep up—especially on stairs, like in train stations. I needed to hold on to the handrails, or to someone's hand. One time I got overtaken by a lady in a traditional Japanese geisha outfit. It was raining and the wet ground affected my balance. She sped right by me in these high wooden platform sandals, while I struggled to stay upright. Slippery floors, uneven surfaces, areas that were not lit properly—all these things would affect my balance.

Being able to gauge my progress between those two trips to Osaka reassured me that improvements were happening, albeit minute ones. It gave me hope that I would be able to get back to some normality one day.

One day I was watching Sydney's City2Surf with a friend in Rose Bay and thought to myself, Wouldn't it be amazing if I could run again—just like I did after my first brain operation back in 2005? I knew that practicing running would improve my walking. I made up my mind I was going to do the fourteen-kilometer run the following year.

I told my personal trainer at the gym what I wanted to do, and he got this concerned look on his face. When we started training, he was at a loss as to how he could help me overcome my challenges. So, the following day, I called the rehabilitation company I had used previously. I told them I wanted a physiotherapist to help me learn to run again. The physio taught me exercises that I could do to help me mimic the motions of a running response, which I then relayed to my gym instructor.

First, we set the target for me to run a hundred meters gracefully. It was a big ask just to do that. My left arm would move out of control when I attempted to run, and smack into my chest and stomach. It was difficult to maintain balance, let alone coordinate my body movements. I couldn't squat as I had no muscle strength in my left leg. I couldn't raise my left foot or stand on my toes. I had no spring in my left foot. I couldn't lift it fast enough—it would slide. My toes would hurt. Regardless of the challenges, I was delighted to be giving it a go.

We had to do these exercises for five months. It wasn't looking good. I could see it in my instructor's eye. He didn't know where all this training was leading. He'd say things like, "When do you reckon you'll stop trying?" and "Should we aim for next year?" He believed in me, but he was quite worried.

After a few months off over the Christmas period, in February 2019, I ran 250 meters without warming up or practicing. A spontaneous Tuesday run. I had a spring in my feet, and my arm was not hurting. My back was not hurting. I was jubilant.

The following Thursday, I was able to run half a kilometer, and by the following week, I ran a pain-free kilometer. Then I ran two kilometers, which was the goal that we'd been practicing for—from the gym in the Rose Bay shops to the police station, around the waterfront track. I even downloaded an app to check my pace. When I reached the police station, I felt victorious—like, "Oh my God, if I can put my mind to this and run, I can do anything!"

I felt like Forrest Gump—so excited about running again. Within a few months, I was running three kilometers, then five, then seven and then from nine to twelve.

I was very happy with my progress and decided to enter the City2Surf. I knew that I probably had about a five percent chance of being able to do it. But that was enough for me to give it all I had.

I was out for a long run one day in May when something happened—I thought I'd torn a muscle. I couldn't extend my legs properly. I didn't think it was anything that serious … I figured if I worked with a physio, I'd soon recover.

The following month I went to the Philippines for work and saw the physio at the gym above our office daily. I kept running as best I could until the pain kicked in. At first, it kicked in about one and a half kilometers in, but as I kept doing laps around the shopping mall each morning, the more laps I could do. Despite the pain, I was improving my speed. The laps around the shopping center were on flat ground, which allowed me to refine my movement and pace significantly.

A month later, I was back in Australia, two weeks out from the race, I was training and felt a pain in my left knee. When I went to have it looked at, scans revealed I had torn the cartilage in my knee because of my imbalanced movement. A few days later I had them scan my hip as well and I had torn the cartilage in my right hip—that's what was causing the pain.

It was game over for the City2Surf—there was no way I could run the race. But it didn't matter because I had proven to myself that I *could* learn to run. I may not have run the race, but I managed to run, which I considered to be a massive achievement. I felt unstoppable.

In August 2019, instead of running in the City2Surf, I was in Osaka for a third time. My running efforts had improved my walking; I was finally walking without difficulty. I was able to carry Billy, who was almost three by then, and drag a bag with wheels while I was walking. I could do this while climbing staircases and on slippery and uneven surfaces, and among crowds. Learning to run had helped me get back to walking with confidence.

Now that I am back to good health, until the VHL tumors kick in once more, I recommitted my full attention to the Remote Staffing business in late 2018. I also invited Rica to work for Remote Staff once again in January 2020 as her remittance business for overseas Filipino workers was getting killed by the Australian banks, which were not providing bank accounts to remittance businesses. This made it difficult for Rica to accept payments from her eighteen thousand customers as she had no bank willing to provide her business with a bank account. In response to this, she partnered with a company, but due to accounting errors and large volumes, it ended up costing half a million dollars. We had to liquidate her business at the end of 2019.

I believe that our business failures—mine with realestate.ph and Rica's with her remittance business—have made us much more mature, more astute, and stronger as a partnership. Actively running the business together once more has been invigorating for both of us. We finally have the capacity to invest in it properly and to see it deliver on its promises to support businesses and Filipino remote workers to reach a new stage of success working together.

Thanks to the COVID pandemic, the outsourcing and offshore staffing industry has exploded in growth around the world. Every day Rica, the team at Remote Staff, and I are committed to taking advantage of this once-in-a-lifetime opportunity to enhance our position in the market and to professionalize the remote working landscape in the Philippines.

Life is great for me after all my operations. I'm living a productive life, purchased my dream home, doubled my wealth, reinvigorated my passion for running my business and enjoying family time with my wife and two sons. I've learned just how strong I really am; I have learned the importance of resilience and how to flourish after each of my adversities. Now, I am looking forward expanding my business across America.

Afterword

My hereditary condition has often humbled me, tested me, and provided me with the ultimate perspective to see my life's challenges in an entirely new way. I'm living on borrowed time, and I don't want to waste it. I have spiritually obligated myself to share my story and to inspire others to accomplish their dreams and to live life fully. As well as to continue employing thousands in remote jobs. The more I can make a meaningful impact in other people's lives, the more I can feel worthy of all my second chances. The more I make my life count while I am alive, the less I worry about how long I live.

I initially started writing this book for my two young sons to know who their father was because I thought I was going to die not long after my brain operation at the age of forty-four. One year later after my brain operation I found myself bargaining for my life and made a pledge to share my story publicly in the hope of inspiring readers like you to continue going after your dreams and to live life fully as I have, despite any adversities.

Living with uncertainty for thirty years has let me cultivate a keen awareness of the present moment, which means I can live deliberately. It has taken me multiple near-death experiences and millions of dollars in business losses to gain a strong mindset. Despite the challenges, I am grateful for all the good things and the bad things—especially this condition I live with, Von Hippel-Lindau syndrome. Without it, I wouldn't have discovered the purposeful and meaningful work I enjoy so much. I might not have been in a position to contribute to other people's lives as much as I am now. I might never have met the woman I love and am married to with two amazing sons. Because of my condition, I never settled into mediocrity.

My mindset has significantly improved my health over multiple extreme adversities. I really can't emphasize that point enough—our mind has the power to heal us. When you can control your mind and develop a strong mindset, you can reinvent yourself, you can change, and you can accomplish one dream after another and improve your odds in overcoming tough times.

So, if your life was affected by COVID or some other extreme challenge, and you're living with some type of mental, emotional, or physical pain, one thing that we can always expect in life—other than death—is change. Even if you don't make any changes, the landscape and the people around you will change over time. It's inevitable. And with change comes healing, so long as you're willing to not hold on to the past. You'll grow, heal, evolve, and become something different. I'm not just talking about weeks or months. I'm talking about years at times. If you can allow years to pass, you can better assess any challenging situation life throws at you with the gift of hindsight. If you're going to give that time to change and be healed from it, you might as well keep the door open for a miracle. Why not? Miracles happen in life and all around us. Why not invite them to happen for you?

Ready to learn the secrets of overcoming obstacles, moving beyond challenges, and creating the life of your dreams? Take a moment to scan this QR code to unlock a free gift that will help you get started on your journey.

Acknowledgments

Special thanks to the team of doctors and medical staff who have helped keep me alive.

I am grateful for the exceptional skills and capability of the surgeons who removed tumors from my brain in two separate operations, first in 2005 and then in 2016.

I greatly appreciate the work of my cancer genetic specialist and her team in helping me understand VHL and how it impacts me and my family. I am grateful for their ongoing support in helping me manage my yearly scans and blood tests.

I am grateful to the urologist who operated on my left kidney twice: first to remove four cancerous tumors in 2008 and the second time to remove six cancerous tumors in 2017. On both occasions, I felt that I needed to bargain for my life, so that I could live for another ten years with my original kidney.